LEAN
TOGETHER

A PUBLICATION OF THE INDEPENDENT WOMEN'S FORUM

LEAN
TOGETHER

AN AGENDA FOR SMARTER GOVERNMENT, STRONGER COMMUNITIES, AND MORE OPPORTUNITY FOR WOMEN

Lean Together: An Agenda for Smarter Government, Stronger Communities, and More Opportunity for Women

Copyright © 2014 Independent Women's Forum

Printed in the United States of America
ISBN-10: 1500182095
ISBN-13: 978-1500182090

Book Cover Design by Michele Vogt
Book Interior Design and Layout by Sekayi A. Stephens

TABLE OF CONTENTS

WHAT'S YOUR VISION FOR AMERICA?

BY CARRIE LUKAS AND SABRINA SCHAEFFER

Ask any woman you know about what she wishes her country and community offered, and we bet you'll find a lot of similarities in what you hear. I want:

A community that is safe and engaged, where people talk to each other and are there to help each other out when someone has a problem.

Plentiful job opportunities for everyone in my family, so that I can find a position that best uses my skills, and gives me flexibility to be with my children or pursue other interests; but also so that teenagers and young-adults have access to the entry-level jobs that are so important for starting careers.

Great educational opportunities and good schools that meet my family's needs as well as those of my neighbors.

A vibrant civil society, where community organizations, charities, and houses of worship can enrich our lives through volunteer opportunities, services, and religious activities—a truly tolerant society where people are free to live out their beliefs.

A robust marketplace, so we can have access to a wide variety of products and foods from around the world at prices we can afford.

A health care system that works so that my family can get the care we need from trusted doctors at a price we can afford. And I want to make sure that this system encourages more life-enhancing treatments and cures for the diseases and ailments that we all face.

A culture that respects both women and men, girls and boys, and encourages the development of healthy relationships and self-images that are the basis for a happy life.

A dependable and accessible safety net so that those who are truly in need get the help they need to get back on their feet. Government plays an important role in this, but so does the rest of the community.

Doesn't this sound like what *you* want? And isn't this what you hear from your friends and neighbors when you talk to them about their concerns about the future and the direction of our country?

This isn't a vision of a go-it-alone society. This is a society that values individual people, families, and the communities they create. It knows that government has an important role to play, and that government needs to perform its duties efficiently and effectively to allow us all to pursue our dreams. But it also recognizes that too much government intrusion can strangle what's best in our communities. This vision recognizes that government largesse can have unintended consequences that discourage the activities and values that are the foundation and core strength of a healthy society.

Too often, progressive activists and Democratic lawmakers present a grim picture of America. They perpetuate the myth that society, our schools, and the workplace are inherently unfair to women and girls today. And they suggest the solution is even more government control and greater dependence on the state by women and their families.

No one can ignore the challenges that many Americans face today. But too many on the Left do ignore the root causes of that hardship. Instead of considering how big government and greater centralization created many of our societal woes, their solution is always more of the same: to double-down on the government-knows-best approach.

The Independent Women's Forum understands that there are real and legitimate difficulties that plague many women and their families, especially unmarried mothers who are more vulnerable to economic hardship. To help solve that problem and ease their burden, we need long-term, sensible solutions and policies that grow our economy, encourage job creation and a more flexible workplace, and increase opportunity for all Americans, women and men alike. We need to be sure Americans of all ages and backgrounds understand the benefits of strong families and communities, and work to create a healthy culture that encourages the best within us. And, just as importantly, we want to make sure our citizens don't have to forfeit their freedoms for government's empty promises.

In this book, you'll hear from a variety of women about issues and policy reforms that can move us in a positive direction toward thriving American communities. They include concrete steps for how our policymakers can institute practical changes—in health care, education, the workplace—in order to bring us in the right direction. Improving the lives of women and their families requires greater educational freedom, fewer taxes and regulations on businesses, a streamlined tax system that allows families to keep more of what they earn, a dynamic marketplace that offers high quality goods at affordable prices, a health care system in which Americans own and control their health care dollars and decisions, and stable families and communities.

It's clear the Left will continue to sell new government programs as gold at the end of the rainbow, and they will forever ignore the very real costs of this intervention on our economy, communities, and families. The impact is not just measured in tax dollars and increased government debt, but in fewer jobs, a less dynamic economy, and less individual freedom. And this over-bearing government is too often women's worst enemy.

That's why we hope you'll find a cause for optimism in these pages: a vision and policy ideas to fight for and to encourage your local representatives and candidates to join you in advancing. No society or government is perfect, but we can certainly do better than we are today. Together, we can make changes to ensure our communities have greater opportunity and the potential for fulfillment. And we can restore the idea that more freedom—not more government—is what will create true health, security, prosperity, and ultimately happiness.

CHAPTER ONE

JOB CREATION IN AMERICA

BY DIANA FURCHTGOTT-ROTH[1]

We want Americans to have a variety of job opportunities. A job gives people a means of support as well as a sense of dignity. A growing economy provides jobs not only to the unemployed, but gives the employed upward mobility by allowing them to change jobs and move up the income ladder. This is true for men, women, and even teens—who frequently choose summer employment if they can get it. A robust job market also means that women are more likely to find a position that makes sense for them in terms of fulfilling other goals, such as balancing work and family responsibilities.

Economic growth is a necessary, but not sufficient, condition for job growth. When demand picks up, employers can choose whether to fill orders by using people or machines. If the government makes it more expensive to hire people, firms will find it profitable to turn to machines rather than hire more workers.

Over the past five years, from 2008 to 2013, the economy has experienced slow growth. In the first quarter of 2014, GDP declined by 2.9 percent.[2] As this volume goes to press in July 2014, the number of payroll jobs in the economy is only 430,000, 3 percent above the level of December 2007, the start of the 2007-2009 recession.[3]

The Labor Department's most frequently used measure of unemployment, U-3, stood at 6.1 percent in June. This does not include discouraged workers, people working part-time when they want full-time jobs, and the underemployed. When these people are included, the Labor Department's broader measure of the unemployment rate, U-6, was 12.1 percent.[4]

Much of the decline in the unemployment rate has been because labor force participation has dropped dramatically since the beginning of the recession and has yet to recover. The labor force participation rate in June was 62.8 percent,[5] equivalent to 1978 levels, before the 1980s when millions of women moved into the labor force. This is down 3 percentage points from 66 percent in December 2007. The share of the unemployed out of work for 27 weeks or longer was 32.8 percent in June, up from 17 percent in December 2007.[6]

The Labor Department's Job Openings and Labor Turnover data also show that hiring has not yet recovered from the recession.[7] The longer people are out of work, the more trouble they have finding jobs afterwards. People out of work for longer periods of time tend to lose hard skills, such as familiarity with the latest technology, and soft skills, such as getting up on time and networking. Training programs for long-term unemployed are more challenging, both for teachers and learners.

Part of the reason for this relatively low job creation is that the Administration has pursued policies that increase the cost of hiring and retaining workers. The Affordable Care Act, signed into law by President Obama in 2010, created new benefit mandates for employers that make employment more costly. Mr. Obama is currently trying to increase it still further by raising the hourly minimum wage from $7.25 to $10.10. When it costs more to hire workers, some firms will expand offshore instead of at home. Others will adjust cash wages down for some employees, and turn to technology to substitute for others, especially at the low-skill end. Some examples are self-scanning machines in retail stores and computerized ordering at restaurants.

A variety of Labor Department proposals would also increase administrative costs for employers, raising the effective cost of employing workers. These include requiring some salaried managers to be paid overtime; requiring overtime to be paid for in-home elderly care; reducing the number of days of campaigns for union representation; and discouraging employers from getting advice on union issues by requiring names of advisors to be made public.

A discussion of all of these proposals is outside the scope of this chapter, but it is important to mention them because they contribute to the government's anti-employment bias and therefore the lack of job growth. If employers see such changes in laws on the horizon, they are likely to reduce hiring plans in the United States in the future.

Data from the Bureau of Economic Analysis show that job growth exists, just not at home. Multinational firms have created more jobs offshore than in the United States. From 2000 to 2011, non-banking multinationals eliminated 2.2 million jobs in the United States, and created 3.4 million jobs overseas.[8] There is no reason—other than counter-productive laws and regulations—that American companies should be turning overseas for workers. Reforming our laws to make it easier and less costly for employers to engage workers in the United States can bring those jobs home, encourage greater economic growth, and create more prosperity for American families.

The remainder of the chapter is divided into two sections. One describes measures the administration could take to increase economic growth, and hence employment. The second shows how employers could be encouraged to hire more workers.

THREE WAYS TO INCREASE ECONOMIC GROWTH

Increase the Efficiency of the Tax System

As is described in more detail in the next chapter, our tax system does not work well. Some say it is broken. Many Americans pay no income taxes; others pay far more than they think reasonable. Ordinary Americans are angry, particularly when there is reason to believe tax administration and enforcement varies by taxpayer.

What can be done to get out of this mess?

Our tax system has three fundamental weaknesses: (1) marginal tax rates are too high; (2) the structures of both personal and corporate taxes are much too complicated; and (3) the incentives for political mischief at the IRS are high, while the likelihood of detection is low. It turns out, all three of these weaknesses are related, and they have one simple solution: tax simplification.

A simpler tax system would solve many problems. It would likely reduce and simplify the benefits of tax-exempt status for all groups, including those targeted by the IRS last year. A simpler tax would also reduce incentives of companies such as Apple to avoid the American tax jurisdiction. But most importantly, tax simplification would stimulate economic growth.

If you want to find complicated taxes, do not look to China. There the economy grows at nearly double-digit rates, and individuals save nearly half of their income, according to noted econometrician and University of Hong Kong professor Lawrence J. Lau, and taxes are less complicated than in America.[9] A complex tax code is not a prerequisite to economic growth, and is in fact the enemy of it.

America's tax system has become so complex that a FY 2014 Taxpayer Advocate Service Report found that 6.1 billion hours per year are spent by individuals and business preparing taxes,[10] not including time spent on audits or responding to IRS notices. All of this is on top of $168 billion spent on tax accountants, lawyers, and filing expenses.

President Obama, Senate Democrats, and House Republicans have all proposed lowering corporate tax rates. Reducing and simplifying corporate taxes would bring in more investment from abroad—together with additional revenue.

America's combined state and federal corporate rate, 39.1 percent, is now the highest in the industrialized world, far above the average of 25.5 percent in the Organisation for Economic Co-operation and Development, our major competitors. Plus, America taxes income on a worldwide rather than territorial basis.

Three examples—Canada, Germany, and the United Kingdom have combined state and federal corporate tax rates of 26 percent, 30 percent, and 23 percent, respectively. All these countries tax corporate income generated only within their borders, rather than corporations' worldwide income, which the United States does. The number of OECD countries with territorial tax systems has more than doubled since 2000, to over 80 percent. Bringing U.S. corporate tax rates in line with worldwide rates will probably bring in revenue and discourage other investments from leaving.

In a November 2013 paper issued by the National Bureau of Economic Research, Professors Kevin Markle of the University of Waterloo and Douglas Shackelford of the University of North Carolina at Chapel Hill concluded that "multinationals headquartered in Japan, the U.S., and some high-tax European countries continue to face substantially higher worldwide taxes than their counterparts in havens and other less heavily taxed locations."[11]

The Senate Permanent Subcommittee on Investigations has estimated that American companies hold around $1.7 trillion of earnings offshore from foreign operations.[12] Some of this would be repatriated with a lower U.S. tax rate or under a territorial system.

Although most agree on the need for corporate tax reform, it will not be easy.

First, Democrats want tax reform to raise revenue, and Republicans regard tax reform as revenue neutral.

Second, with lower corporate rates, the difference in rates between small businesses—who file under the individual tax schedule with top rates of 39.6 percent—would widen. Ideally, rates should be identical, so that all entities face the same rates. Some businesses currently subject to individual income taxes would incorporate to get lower rates if the corporate code was reformed.

Third, capital-intensive corporations such as automobile manufacturers would likely lose some deductions with lower tax rates. Tax reform would help service and financial industries, but could result in a tax increase on manufacturers.

However, as a part of reform, Congress could allow immediate, first-year write offs of plant and equipment for corporations and small businesses. This would bring our current tax system closer to a consumption tax— under which income that is saved or invested is not taxed—and generate much-needed new investment in plant and equipment.

High rates and complexity discourage even the most earnest taxpayers. The solution is to simplify the tax code.

Encourage Development of Fossil Fuels

Everyone knows where the jobs are—North Dakota, with a 2.7 percent unemployment rate in June 2014, the lowest in the nation. And everyone knows why—the New American Energy Revolution is bringing previously-unrecoverable oil and natural gas out of the ground with a novel technology, hydraulic fracturing. As described in more detail in chapter eight, North America may become a natural gas exporter by 2020, according to the International Energy Agency, and a net energy exporter by 2035.[13]

And everyone knows where the jobs aren't—alternative energy, even though solar, wind, and biofuels have received billions in government loans and grants. The list of bankrupt companies that have received government funding includes: Solyndra ($528 million from Uncle Sam), Abound Solar ($400 million), Beacon Power ($43 million), and A123 ($249 million), to name just a few.

But the administration is bringing out new regulations on hydraulic fracturing that could stem the New American Energy Revolution. The Energy Department, the Interior Department, the Environmental Protection Agency, even the Securities and Exchange Commission, all have regulations in development. President Obama has refused to approve Keystone XL, the pipeline that would bring oil from Canada to refineries near the Gulf.

Manhattan Institute scholar Mark Mills concluded in a February 2014 paper that the energy revolution has been America's biggest creator of jobs, in occupations ranging from construction to services to information technology.[14] Almost one million Americans across the United States are employed directly in the oil and gas industry, and 10 million jobs are linked to oil and gas.

Import Immigrants

As America seeks to increase economic growth, immigration reform should be part of the growth agenda. If it were easier for foreign-born students and workers to obtain provisional visas to stay and work in America, visas that could transition into green cards later, America would have faster GDP growth and job creation.

Immigrants are prominent in advanced scientific research. Over one-third of U.S. Nobel Prize winners between 1901 and 2013 were foreign-born. Highly-skilled immigrants are disproportionately represented in successful startups. They benefit the United States because they found new companies in America at greater rates than do native-born residents.

Dartmouth University professor Matthew Slaughter estimates that America is losing 2,000 jobs a day, or a job every 43 seconds, by capping H-1B visas to skilled immigrants at 85,000. He calculates that 100,000 jobs are lost directly from unfiled H-1B visa applications, and 400,000 jobs are lost indirectly because they are not generated by the innovators.[15]

Immigrants are also needed at the low end of the skill scale. Farms provide income to farmers, as well as to other native-born Americans employed in the trucking and distribution industries. If farmers cannot get low-skill immigrants to pick fruit, as was the case in Washington State for the 2012 apple crop, agriculture will move offshore to where low-skill labor can be found. It makes little sense to send a whole economic sector to other countries just to avoid employing immigrants.

THREE WAYS TO INCREASE HIRING

In addition to promoting economic growth broadly, policymakers can encourage job creation by making it easier for employers to hire and retain workers.

Repeal Employer Penalties for Obamacare

The Affordable Care Act is making hiring more expensive. Employers with more than 49 but less than 100 full-time workers who do not offer the right kind of health insurance will face penalties of $2,000 per full-time worker per year, beginning in 2016. For firms with 100 or more full-time employees, the penalties begin in 2015. A firm that expands from 49 to 50 workers could face a tax of $40,000 per year (the first 30 workers are exempt).

Many firms around 45 full-time employees are reconsidering expansion, and some just over the limit are considering moving employees to part-time to avoid the penalty. Firms also have an added incentive to become more automated, to use more machinery, and employ fewer workers. The Obama Administration knows there will be negative employment effects to ObamaCare. That is why the President continues to change the Act and delay the starting date of penalties.

The solution: stop requiring employers to offer healthcare. Food, clothing and housing are equally important, but government does not require employers to provide them. There are better ways to help Americans obtain affordable high quality health care (as is discussed in more detail in chapter three) without discouraging employment by creating new burdens on employers. A tax on employment, such as a $2,000 penalty for failing to offer adequate health insurance, will always result in fewer people hired.

Lower the Minimum Wage Rather than Raising It

The losers of the push to raise the hourly federal minimum wage from $7.25 to $10.10 are the young and unskilled, who will be unable to join the labor market and get their feet on the first rungs of the career ladder. Rather than raise the wage, Congress should lower it.

In a global economy, where competitive countries battle for business with well-trained, disciplined, and experienced employees, America is putting itself at a disadvantage by keeping young Americans off the first rung of the career ladder.

Make no mistake—few workers stay at the minimum wage level very long. Only three percent of American workers earn the minimum wage.

The other 97 percent make more, not because of government regulation, but because that is the only way that employers can persuade them to stay.

University of California (Berkeley) professors Michael Reich and Ken Jacobs have concluded that the $13 per hour minimum compensation package in San Francisco did not adversely affect employment in the city.[16] That could be because firms replaced low-skill employees with high-skill workers.

Yet California's economy is doing poorly in comparison to others and other studies suggest there is a relationship between a higher minimum wage and fewer jobs. It is one of the states with the highest unemployment rates, along with Rhode Island, Nevada, Illinois, and Michigan. In June 2014, these highest rates ranged from 7.9 percent in Rhode Island to 7.1 percent in Illinois. All have state minimum wage laws that are higher than the federal wage law. California's unemployment was 7.4 percent in June 2014, the fifth highest unemployment rate in America. Internal Revenue Service data compiled by the non-partisan Tax Foundation reveal that from 2000 to 2010 California lost a net $29.4 billion in adjusted gross income and 1.2 million residents to other states.[17]

It is noteworthy that of the five states with the lowest unemployment rates at the start of 2014 (North Dakota, Nebraska, South Dakota, Utah, and Vermont), only one, Vermont, has a minimum wage that is higher than the federal minimum wage. The unemployment rates ranged from 2.7 percent in North Dakota to 3.8 percent in South Dakota. In May the national unemployment rate was 6.3 percent.

University of California (Irvine) professor David Neumark, in a paper forthcoming in the Industrial and Labor Relations Review, writes that the strongest evidence linking unemployment to increases in the minimum wage suggests that teenagers and other low-skill groups, without regard to industry, are the most likely groups to be adversely affected.[18]

A February 2014 Congressional Budget Office study shows that approximately 500,000 low-skilled people would lose their jobs by 2016 due to a proposed increase in the federal minimum wage to $10.10 from $7.25.[19]

In March 2014, 500 economists, including Nobel laureates Vernon Smith, Eugene Fama, Robert Lucas, and Edward Prescott, signed a letter opposing increases in the federal minimum wage. "Although increasing wages through legislative action may sound like a great idea, poverty is a serious, complex issue that demands a comprehensive and thoughtful solution that targets those Americans actually in need," they wrote.[20]

If you were running a business, and the minimum wage rose from $7.25 to $10.10, your first step would be to lay off your least-skilled workers. Future workers would have to produce more in order to earn a position. You might do less on-the-job training and hire workers who already have experience.

Rather than a federal minimum wage, states should be allowed to set their own wage levels. Some might decide not to have any minimum wage at all. With the cost of living varying dramatically between states, what makes sense for New York might not work in Alabama.

Reform Entitlements

The proportion of working-age Americans who have jobs or who are looking for them has been falling, even though employment has been expanding, albeit fitfully and at a sluggish pace.

It is understandable that people drop out of the labor force—stop looking for work—when unemployment is rising and they have become discouraged. But, since the employment rebound from the 2007-2009 recession began in March 2010, the labor-force participation rate has fallen for both men and women. This appears to be part of a long decline that dates from 2000.

One reason for this trend, which appears to be continuing, is the panoply of government benefits, including unemployment insurance, which only recently reverted back to 26 weeks in most states—the standard, pre-recession length. Other elements of the federal safety net include food stamps, mortgage relief, and Temporary Assistance to Needy Families. The provision of subsidized healthcare for those earning below 400 percent of the poverty line under the Affordable Care Act, beginning in 2014, will exacerbate this.

Casey B. Mulligan, an economics professor at the University of Chicago, has shown that benefits account for half the decline in the labor force participation rate.[21] He examines how increases in benefits have discouraged people from working by raising marginal tax rates among recipients. As beneficiaries lose their eligibility for benefits by working, the loss of these benefits has the same effect as a tax.

These programs have expanded in two ways. Eligibility has increased, and the programs have become more generous.

Take unemployment insurance. Between 2007 and 2010, when the country was in deep recession and gradual recovery, spending on unemployment insurance rose by 293 percent adjusted for inflation, Mulligan calculates. If unemployment eligibility and benefit rules had remained at 2007 levels, spending would have risen by 50 percent.

Mulligan explains that when unemployment insurance pays more, "the reward to working declines, because some of the money earned on the job is now available even when not working. Decades of empirical economic research show that the reward to working, as determined by the safety net and other factors, affects how many people work and how many hours they work."

CONCLUSION

The defining challenge of our time is reversing the decline in labor force participation and creating more jobs. To reverse this trend, policymakers must focus on ways to encourage economic growth by facilitating business growth and investment, lower the barriers to job creation for employers, and make employment more attractive to potential workers. Such policies will help both men and women, now and in the future.

CHAPTER TWO

TAXES AND SPENDING: MORE THAN DOLLARS AND CENTS

BY ROMINA BOCCIA

mericans deserve a government budget that uses taxpayer dollars wisely, prioritizes properly, and doesn't create an unsupportable debt for the next generation. Americans also deserve a tax system that is easy to understand, treats people fairly, and doesn't discourage productive behaviors or impede economic growth. Americans know that a functioning, stable federal government with a budget reasonably balanced is necessary for our economy to function and for individuals to prosper.

Unfortunately today, Washington's tax and budget policies aren't living up to this vision, and hard-working American families are bearing their costs. Spending and taxes are on the rise. Deficits and debt are projected to reach historically unprecedented and economically dangerous levels. Younger generations—from today's toddlers to college students—are at risk of inheriting a weaker economy overburdened with excessive levels of debt. The federal budget is in dire need of reform.

Women know particularly well what it takes to make a household budget work. Women control about 75 percent of household spending.[1] American families strive to be responsible with their family budget, paying down their debts and setting aside savings for rainy days, their children's college, and their own retirement. They have a rightful expectation that their elected representatives will emulate them in the public realm.

When Americans hear that Congress is running massive and chronic deficits with no end in sight, and at the same time they are told that there is nothing that could possibly be cut from the bloated federal budget, it's frustrating to say the least.[2] It is especially so, considering that America's tax burden is also going up, yet the deficit persists. The $17 trillion national debt, the result of several decades of deficit spending, raises concerns for the future of America's children and grandchildren.[3] It hangs like a dark cloud over the American economy, and yet Congress is doing little to control it.

Comparing the federal government to a family budget illustrates the extent of the federal government's irresponsibility. As shown in this graph, were a median-income family to spend and borrow like the federal government, they would be in a world of trouble.

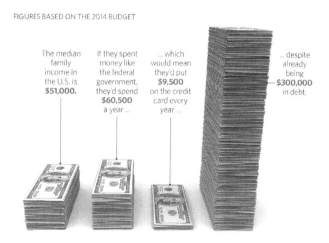

What if a Typical Family Spent and Borrowed Like the Federal Government?

Families understand that it is unwise to repeatedly spend much more than they take in. But Washington continues its shopping spree on the taxpayer credit card with seemingly no regard to the stack of bills the nation has already piled up.

FIGURES BASED ON THE 2014 BUDGET

The median family income in the U.S. is **$51,000.**

If they spent money like the federal government, they'd spend **$60,500** a year ...

... which would mean they'd put **$9,500** on the credit card every year ...

... despite already being **$300,000** in debt.

Source: Congressional Budget Office

Fix the Debt Chart 2 • Federal Budget in Pictures 2014 heritage.org

TAKING CONTROL OF THE BUDGET

The first step to taking control of a budget is figuring out how much money is currently being spent and where that money is going. Next we need to define spending properly, separating the necessary from the discretionary, and set priorities. Policymakers need to develop and implement a fair, transparent tax system that raises revenue sufficient to provide for government's spending. And the last step is sticking to that budget, paying down debt, and planning for the future. This is true for a family budget as much as for the federal budget.

The federal government is supposed to use taxpayer money to advance the public interest as delineated by the Constitution. Foremost, the federal government is charged with providing for the national defense. A strong national defense is necessary to defend individual liberty, political freedom, the U.S., its people and assets against foreign threats, and to live up to the nation's global security commitments.[4]

Beyond defending the nation, according to the Constitution, the federal government is supposed to play a very limited role in American life, leaving most decisions to the private sector and Americans at the state and local level. This is for very good reasons. The interest of the public is best reflected when decisions are made at the closest, most local level possible.

We know how this works when it comes to individuals. Individuals are best suited to know their own preferences, and the private sector competes and innovates to provide more and higher quality goods and services at the lowest cost possible to meet those preferences, making all Americans better off in the process.

Policy decisions should also be made at the most local level possible. State and local government decision-making allows for competition among policies and provides constituents with greater chances for involvement in the process. Unlike the case with national policies, constituents can move to another jurisdiction if they disagree with the chosen policies. Areas such as infrastructure, police, education, and environmental protection are best handled privately, or on a state and local level with little to no interference from bureaucrats in Washington. One-size-fits-all solutions often cause more problems than they solve. States and localities are much better able to find unique solutions that suit their constituents.

To pay for federal spending, the government should strive for a tax system that raises the needed resources while minimizing the tax system's impact on individual economic decisions. This means that it should be easy for people to figure out how much taxes they owe and to pay those taxes in a straightforward manner. Taxes should not influence how much people spend versus save, and the tax system should be fair towards lenders and borrowers. This also means that no industry should receive special tax advantages that aren't available to everyone else. The tax system should be simple and fair to all Americans.

This is not the kind of budget the U.S. keeps today. The federal government is overextended in many areas, encroaching upon decisions that are best made by individuals in society, not by Washington bureaucrats. The tax code is overly complex and bestows special benefits upon certain well-connected groups in society, while discouraging savings and work. Americans deserve better.

WHERE THE MONEY GOES

Less than one-fifth of the federal government's spending goes towards protecting America from foreign threats and securing U.S. national interests abroad. Spending on the largest entitlement programs—Social Security, Medicare, Medicaid, and other health programs—already consumes almost half of the federal budget. Unless reformed, these entitlements will devour 75 cents of every dollar in tax revenue collected within one generation.[5] Other federal income security programs, like unemployment and disability benefits together with federal employee retirement benefits, consume another fifth of the budget. In all, about two-thirds of spending is considered a transfer from taxpayers to groups of eligible beneficiaries.[6]

Where Does All the Money Go?

In 2013, the major entitlement programs—Social Security, Medicare, Medicaid, and other health care—consumed 49 percent of all federal spending. These programs, and interest on the debt, are on track to consume an even greater share of spending in future years, while the portion of federal spending dedicated to other national priorities will decline.

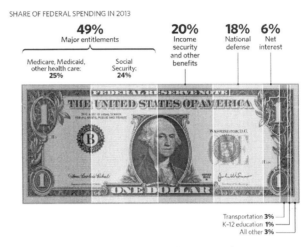

SHARE OF FEDERAL SPENDING IN 2013

49% Major entitlements

Medicare, Medicaid, other health care: **25%** Social Security: **24%**

20% Income security and other benefits

18% National defense

6% Net interest

Transportation **3%**
K–12 education **1%**
All other **3%**

Source: Office of Management and Budget. Note: Income security and other benefits includes federal employee retirement and disability, unemployment compensation, veterans benefits, food and housing assistance, and other federal income security programs.

Cut Spending Chart 1 • Federal Budget in Pictures 2014 ☎ heritage.org

Defense is part of the one-third of the federal budget that is considered discretionary spending; meaning Congress has to authorize it each and every year. The process of authorizing spending is itself important, affording members of Congress an opportunity to debate which programs should receive funding in any given year, and how much they should receive.

Unfortunately this debate does not always happen. More often than not, Congress will simply authorize spending to continue as before, using a mechanism called a continuing resolution. Another method with which Congress avoids budget debate is to assemble all spending into one massive bill, called an Omnibus, which spans over a thousand pages and is brought to the floor within only a few short days of an impending government shutdown. To no one's surprise, few if any members of Congress read omnibus bills or raise specific objections.[7]

The vastly larger part of the budget—two-thirds of federal spending— grows on autopilot, and receives little to no congressional attention. This is called mandatory spending. These programs receive funding based on past authorizations and can undergo no changes over decades.

The last time Congress made changes to Social Security was thirty years ago. With almost no regular congressional deliberation, it is no wonder that mandatory spending is the key driver of our deficit and long-term debt problem. If Congress does nothing, spending on the major entitlement programs and interest on the debt will consume all tax revenues in less than one generation.[8]

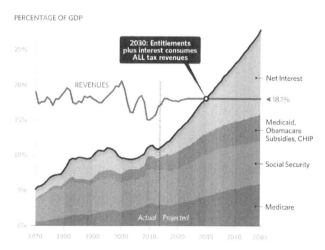

All Tax Revenue Will Go Toward Entitlements and Net Interest by 2030

In less than two decades, all projected tax revenues would be consumed by three federal programs (Medicare, Social Security, and Medicaid, which includes CHIP and Obamacare) and interest on the debt. Entitlement reform is a must.

PERCENTAGE OF GDP

2030: Entitlements plus interest consumes ALL tax revenues

REVENUES

Net Interest

◄ 18.1%

Medicaid, Obamacare Subsidies, CHIP

Social Security

Medicare

Actual | Projected

25%   20%   15%   10%   5%   0%

1970   1980   1990   2000   2010   2020   2030   2040   2040

Sources: Congressional Budget Office and Office of Management and Budget.

Fix the Debt Chart 6 • Federal Budget in Pictures 2014 ☎ heritage.org

This spending tsunami is a major threat to limited government because entitlement spending increases automatically each year based on each program's governing laws. Entitlements get the first call on tax revenues; other priorities, such as defense or national security, must make due with an increasingly smaller share of whatever is left. This supposedly "locked in" spending is steadily undermining other national priorities and threatens the economic future of younger generations.

ENTITLEMENT REFORM TO PRESERVE ECONOMIC SECURITY

Entitlement program spending is on track to single-handedly bankrupt the nation and reduce economic growth in the future. Younger generations are faced with a massive and growing debt burden from unaffordable spending on Social Security, Medicare, Medicaid, and ObamaCare benefits.

Decades ago, Washington politicians promised baby boomers health and retirement benefits that we now cannot afford because they did not design the programs in a way that protected taxpayers from their ever-increasing costs. Now we are faced with the consequences of their neglect. America's public debt is three-quarters the size of the nation's economic product and is growing rapidly.

Moreover, unsustainable entitlement financing puts America's most vulnerable populations at risk of seeing their benefits reduced steeply and abruptly by forced austerity. Entitlement programs play the crucial role of keeping especially elderly and disabled Americans out of poverty.

Social Security, Medicare, and Medicaid could be unable to fulfill this important role in the not too distant future if lawmakers continue to neglect their unsustainable financing. Women are particularly at risk. Non-married women are almost twice as likely to retire in poverty, with 15.5 percent being poor, compared to the average among all Social Security recipients of 8.9 percent.[9]

Meanwhile, unfunded liabilities in Medicare and Social Security far surpass the level of debt the government recognizes in its financial report. Medicare ($36.2 trillion) and Social Security ($12.3 trillion) face almost $48.5 trillion in long-term unfunded obligations. We must begin now to address these shortfalls. The Congressional Budget Office estimates that without fiscal restraint, public debt could exceed an economically harmful 100 percent of GDP by 2028—within less than one generation.

On top of the massive financing issues of the current entitlement programs, individual Americans and the economy at large now also face the burden of ObamaCare. The Patient Protection and Affordable Care Act was enacted in 2010 and is expected to cost $1.8 trillion by 2023. Full implementation of its new entitlements began in 2014.

The moral challenge created by entitlement spending is undermining our democratic system as more Americans become dependent on the government and other priorities are automatically preempted. It also presents a moral challenge in that current generations are indebting younger and future generations. Counting the current debt and unfunded obligations in Medicare and Social Security, today's Americans face a debt burden of more than $220,000 per person. Congress can provide a durable safety net without bankrupting younger generations and the nation. There's a way, if only there was a will.

To protect vulnerable Americans from poverty, Congress should transform the entitlement programs away from unaffordable social insurance benefits for everyone regardless of need, toward a real insurance model that provides a durable safety net for Americans. Individuals can help solve the budget challenge also, by providing for more of their foreseeable retirement needs through personal savings and insurance. These steps will ensure a fiscally sustainable future and better stewardship for younger generations.

WHERE DOES OUR GOVERNMENT'S MONEY COME FROM?

More than 45 percent of all federal tax revenue comes from the individual income tax.[10] Despite populist rhetoric to the contrary, wealthier Americans carry the vast majority of the federal income tax burden. In 2010, the top 10 percent of income earners paid 71 percent of all federal income taxes, while earning 45 percent of all income. In a comparison with other industrialized nations, the U.S. is the most progressive in terms of taxation.[11]

Top 10 Percent of Earners Paid 68 Percent of Federal Income Taxes

Top earners are the main target of tax increases, but the federal income tax system is already highly progressive. The top 10 percent of income earners paid 68 percent of all federal income taxes in 2011 while earning 45 percent of all income. The bottom 50 percent paid 3 percent of income taxes but earned 12 percent of income.

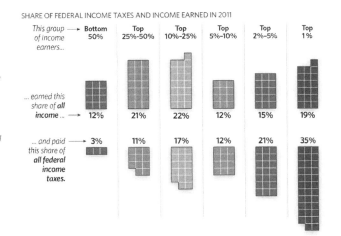

SHARE OF FEDERAL INCOME TAXES AND INCOME EARNED IN 2011

This group of income earners...	Bottom 50%	Top 25%-50%	Top 10%-25%	Top 5%-10%	Top 2%-5%	Top 1%
... earned this share of **all income** ...	12%	21%	22%	12%	15%	19%
... and paid this share of **all federal income taxes.**	3%	11%	17%	12%	21%	35%

Source: Internal Revenue Service. Note: Figures do not sum to totals due to rounding.

Reduce the Tax Burden Chart 1 • Federal Budget in Pictures 2014 ☎ heritage.org

Even though the bottom 50 percent of income earners paid only 2 percent of federal income taxes, they carry a larger share of the payroll tax burden. Payroll taxes, identified on a worker's paycheck as FICA taxes, are dedicated to the Social Security and Medicare programs. About 35 percent of all federal income taxes are payroll taxes.[12]

Corporate income taxes bring in another 10 percent. Corporate profits are double-taxed. First, corporations pay tax on their profits, and when those profits are distributed to shareholders, the same profits are taxed again as dividends. This is one reason why many economists argue that corporate taxes should be reduced, if not eliminated. While this may sound counter-intuitive, lower corporate taxes would benefit workers the most in the form of more jobs and higher wages.[13]

The remaining 10 percent comes in part from excise taxes, those collected on specific sales like the gas tax, and from a hodgepodge of other taxes, such as the death tax, gift taxes, and customs taxes.[14]

A SIMPLER, FAIRER TAX SYSTEM

Ideally, taxes should raise the revenue to fund necessary government operations in a manner that causes the least economic damage. An overly complex tax code built on high tax rates and filled with needless and harmful loopholes is unfair to Americans and hurts economic growth. Sadly, that's what we have today.

The current tax code imposes huge compliance burdens on individuals and businesses, who lose an estimated 6.1 billion hours complying with IRS filing requirements at a cost of more than $100 billion.[15]

Congress should adopt a pro-growth, job-creating tax reform plan that simplifies our tax system and facilitates economic growth. This would unlock opportunities for middle-class and low-income families to better provide for themselves and improve their standard of living. Tax reform done right is a way to improve opportunity for those who are struggling to get ahead in today's economy, and plays an important role in providing the funds to pay for national priorities since a growing economy is the best way to generate sufficient federal revenue.

High tax rates discourage the very productive activities that are the basis of economic growth. Working, saving, investing, and entrepreneurship are all affected by how the government chooses to tax. When taxes are too high and favor certain groups of well-connected Americans over others, it hurts growth and prevents the economy from reaching its full potential. The tax code is littered with too many politically motivated credits, deductions, and exemptions that only serve to further inhibit economic growth.

Unfortunately the debate over tax reform has been diverted by those who view it as another way for Washington to end up with more of the taxpayers' hard-earned income. Tax reform should make the tax code simpler and fairer for all Americans, and it should promote economic growth and opportunity. Tax reform should not be a euphemism for tax increases, by expanding the share of taxpayers' resources that flows into Washington.

The good news is that tax reform does not have to increase the burden of government on Americans to achieve the same or even higher amounts of revenue for Washington. The best predictor of how much revenue

Washington can collect is the direction of the overall economy. If fewer people are unemployed, then more Americans are able to earn higher wages (and pay taxes). And if more businesses are able to expand and bring new and more efficient products to market, then Washington is able to collect more revenue without distorting those very activities. In fact, a simpler and fairer tax code could result in a future tax cut as pro-growth tax reform grows the economic pie and tax revenues.

One of the best ways to make the tax code much, much simpler is to adopt a consumption-based tax, like one flat tax rate. While the number of countries that have adopted a flat tax over the past decade has quadrupled, the U.S. recently went in the opposite direction and added an additional tax bracket instead.[16] The U.S. now has seven different tax brackets to collect income taxes from individuals, families, and many small businesses. In a flat tax system, there would only be one tax bracket. This would make it much easier for a taxpayer to figure out what they owe. And because everyone would face the same tax rate, the system would be fair to all taxpayers.

The U.S. payroll tax system operates like a flat tax in some respects. Up to $117,000 in income, every income earner pays 6.2 percent in payroll taxes to Social Security (their employer also pays 6.2 percent). Someone earning $10,000 would pay $620 in payroll taxes and someone earning $100,000 would pay $6,200. A flat tax is easy and fair to all Americans.

The tax code should also avoid double-taxation as is the case with savings in the U.S. today. Dividends, interest on savings, and capital gains are double-taxed in the U.S., which discourages savings and investment. By taxing all income only once as earned income, the new system would eliminate the current bias against saving and investing and unleash economic growth.

Moreover, tax reform should begin from the assumption that all tax loopholes and special exemptions and deductions should be eliminated from the start. Congress should only add back in those that make broad sense in the context of minimizing economic distortions as much as possible.[17]

The U.S. corporate tax system also needs reform. The U.S. has the highest corporate income tax rate in the industrialized world—almost 40 percent when the federal rate is combined with the average corporate state tax. Businesses wanting to make new investments and create jobs face the highest tax rate in the U.S. Much like the individual tax code, the corporate tax system is riddled with loopholes and special tax exemptions.

The U.S. corporate rate should be transparent and simple and allow the U.S. to be competitive with other industrialized nations. As mentioned in the previous chapter, the average corporate tax rate among the Organisation for Economic Co-operation and Development members is 25 percent. In order to be internationally competitive as a place where businesses want to locate and expand their operations, the U.S. should adopt a corporate rate at or below the OECD average.

A simpler and fairer tax code would unleash economic growth and job creation in the U.S., helping all Americans by providing them with greater opportunities for jobs, higher wages, and investments.

ON A PATH TO FISCAL RESPONSIBILITY AND ECONOMIC GROWTH

The need for budget and tax reform is clear. Less clear is what a path to fiscal responsibility and greater economic growth would look like. Most spending and taxing decisions are not made within the context of thorough congressional deliberation. Rather, special interests are driving politics in America at the expense of the interests of the general public and the American taxpayer. To truly reform America's budget, lawmakers have to bind themselves with rules that, if violated, carry painful consequences. Moreover, rules should be simple so they can be understood by a watchful public to help hold lawmakers accountable.

Here is an agenda for America to improve the nation's fiscal and economic future:

- **Reform Entitlement Programs:** Lawmakers' failure
  to reform the nation's critical entitlement programs

is unfair to younger generations and puts the livelihoods of the elderly and the poor at risk. By focusing entitlement benefits on those who actually need them, lawmakers can avoid indiscriminate cuts to entitlement benefits. Lawmakers should also put entitlements on a budget that requires congressional action at least every five years. This would encourage important benefit reforms like gradually increasing the retirement age with increases in life expectancy and reducing unaffordable benefit increases, before drastic changes become necessary to ward off bankruptcy. With the right reforms, Congress can protect America's most vulnerable populations by providing a durable safety net, without burdening younger generations with economically harmful debt levels or higher taxes.

- **Reform the Tax Code:** America's needlessly complex tax code is a drag on economic growth and job creation. Special tax loopholes and deductions also make the tax code unfair. The key to improving the tax code is to simplify it by eliminating deductions and other loop holes, while reducing tax rates. Ultimately, the goal should be for the United States to have one flat rate with very limited deductions to minimize the impact the tax code has on individual economic decisions. This would unleash economic growth and provide greater opportunities for middle-income and low-income Americans to provide a better living standard for their families.

   The corporate tax rate should also be radically simplified, eliminating special treatment for industries. This would allow policymakers to dramatically cut our highest-in-the world corporate tax rate so that

American companies can compete head on with other industrialized nations for business investment and job creation here at home.

A simpler, more transparent, and less burdensome tax code would be a boon to economic growth and American prosperity.

- **Eliminate Waste, Duplication, and Inappropriate Federal Spending:** The most commonsense way to move toward a balanced budget is to stop overspending. There is a great deal of waste that can be cut from the federal budget to reduce spending. From $5 million spent on fancy crystal in the State Department, to a single $1 million bus stop in the Washington area, to a luxury trip to the Caribbean for federal employees for which taxpayers have yet to get clarity on its cost, the federal government knows how to spend money irresponsibly.[18] Greater oversight and financial transparency would go a long way in reining in lavish agency spending.

  Moreover, reducing improper payments through better oversight and management could save billions every year. The Federal government wasted more than $100 billion in 2012 alone by making improper payments, such as sending checks to people who should not receive them, overpaying for medical equipment or paying for goods and services that were never delivered, as well as paying benefits to dead people. The vast bulk of improper payments happen in federal health care programs, where government intervention has grown rapidly. Moving towards a market-based, patient-centered approach to health care (as described in more detail in the next chapter) would help beneficiaries and taxpayers tremendously.

In addition, each year, the Government Accountability Office releases a report detailing duplication among federal government agencies, along with recommendations on how to fix the problem.[19] Having this information available is the first step. Especially in times of tight budgets as is the case when Congress imposes a firm spending cap, some agencies take the GAO's recommendations to heart. But too many don't, which is where Congressional oversight committees should come in to tie agency funding to improvements in the management of taxpayer resources. Congress also should play a role in that many GAO-identified actions require congressional authorization, like preventing individuals from double-dipping from unemployment and disability benefits. A specifically dedicated, independent commission with the charge to eliminate waste, and consolidate duplicative programs, could help Congress accomplish these goals.[20]

Such a commission should also be charged with identifying government programs that unfairly compete with the private sector, or that should be within the purview of state and local government. Reining in the federal government as it encroaches on more spheres that are not national priorities is key to reducing the power of Washington bureaucrats to meddle in affairs better left to individuals, businesses, and state and local government.

- **Enact and Enforce Firm Spending Caps.** Firm spending caps would encourage lawmakers to allocate scarce resources towards their greatest uses, by prioritizing federal spending based on constitutional principles. Spending caps enable lawmakers to say no to special interests and protect American taxpayers from wasteful spending burdens. Spending caps could be implemented in a number of different ways. For example:

Spend One Dollar Less. This rule would require Congress to spend just one dollar less next year than they did this year. This rule could be especially effective with the part of the budget that funds federal agencies and programs anew each year, allowing Congress to freeze the budget minus one dollar. Today, spending goes up every year in part to account for changes in the cost of living, or inflation. Spend one dollar less each year would result in a much bigger effective cut in spending after adjusting for inflation. This would significantly reduce the size of government over time.

Limit Spending Growth to Inflation. This approach would increase spending in real dollar terms to make up for changes in inflation. Instead of reducing the effective size of government, this rule would stop government from growing more rapidly by keeping the government's purchasing power constant.

Limit Spending Growth to Economic Growth. Measuring the size of government in terms of the economy, through gross-domestic product (GDP), shows how big government is compared with measured private sector activity. This rule would bind government so that it can grow no faster than the economy. While such a rule would be an improvement over unlimited spending increases, it implicitly assumes that when the economy grows, government should grow as well. Limiting the growth in government spending to the growth in the economy would help limit the size of government to what Americans can afford. But being able to afford bigger and more intrusive government does not mean that this is the wisest choice.[21]

- **Control the Debt.** High public debt poses a moral challenge and hurts economic growth. The nation's first President, George Washington, suggested that Congress should avoid "the accumulation of debt" so as to "not ungenerously [throw] upon posterity the burden which we ourselves ought to bear." Debt is a result of consuming future resources today. When taxpayers today receive government benefits that their generation does not pay for, it robs younger generations of future resources and leaves them with a higher tax burden. Some argue that deficit-spending is an investment in the future and that younger generations will reap the benefits in the form of higher growth, better roads, advances in scientific research, etc. Some government spending today may indeed bring future benefits, but today the federal government has become so bloated and overextended that it is difficult to argue that this deficit-spending is really a worthy investment for future taxpayers. Instead, the growing debt will deliver less growth and fewer opportunities for tomorrow's taxpayers.

  Consider a recent study by economists at the International Monetary Fund, which found that the economies of high-debt nations (defined as those with debt above 90 percent of GDP) grew 1.3 percentage points slower than their low-debt counterparts (debt less than 30 percent of GDP), and the effect gets worse as debt grows higher. Heritage Foundation economist, Salim Furth, Ph.D., calculated the impact on American families and found that by the year 2023, lower growth from high debt would leave the typical American family $11,000 poorer thanit would otherwise be.[22]

Congress can control the debt in a number of ways:

Cut Spending Before Increasing the Debt Limit. A vote to increase the debt ceiling is a highly public affair and an opportunity to hold Congress and the President accountable for failing to control spending and waste and for authorizing money for pork projects. Importantly, the debt limit allows Congress to exercise its power of the purse in making vital course corrections when confronted with the results of unsustainable spending decisions. As such, the debt limit presents a decisive, action-forcing moment for Congress. Congress should cut current and future spending before increasing the debt limit.

Adopt a Debt Brake. During economic downturns, revenue collected from taxes drops significantly as businesses are able to sell fewer goods and fewer Americans are able to find and keep jobs. Spending on safety net programs like unemployment insurance also rises steeply during downturns, resulting in temporary deficits even for otherwise responsible nations. To limit spending and the deficit while allowing for flexibility during temporary economic downturns, Switzerland and Germany adopted a constitutional "debt brake." The brake limits the size of the deficit over a period of time, allowing the government to run up bigger deficits during times of economic distress by making up for such deficits with surpluses in better years. The U.S. might consider adopting a debt brake to limit spending and deficits.

Adopt a Balanced Budget Amendment. Supporters of the Balanced Budget Amendment want to force the federal government through a constitutional requirement to live within its means— to spend no more than it takes in. Recent analysis by F.F. Wiley of 63 high debt episodes in history show that large countries that reduced their debt without experiencing a credit-related crisis all did so by balancing their budget. In the authors' words, "history suggests that the only reliable way to solve a debt problem is to stop running deficits."[23]

An effective Balanced Budget Amendment must control spending, taxation, and borrowing; ensure the defense of the nation; and enforce the requirement to balance the budget through the legislative process. Moreover, a BBA should have certain emergency provisions that allow for flexibility in the event that a major economic crisis or a war requires temporary borrowing, similar to the rules that apply to the European debt brake.

The states show how a balanced budget rule could work as well as how it can sometimes be circumvented—providing important lessons for federal lawmakers.

SECURING THE BLESSINGS OF LIBERTY

Federal spending is too high and too much of it is wasted and poorly targeted. In 2012 alone, Washington wasted at least $100 billion in improper payments.[24] While the nation's military forces and readiness programs are being cut, mandatory spending is growing uncontrolled. Lawmakers' fiscal recklessness is unfair to current and future Americans who bear the burden of high and inefficient taxation in addition to growing debt. Younger generations are particularly harmed by high levels of deficit spending and debt, which threaten to reduce economic growth and their opportunities to achieve prosperity in America in the future.

American families strive to live within their means and to provide their children with a better future than they enjoyed. America's Founders envisioned the nation's elected officials exercising similar prudence and enshrined the following goal in the preamble to the U.S. Constitution: "to secure the Blessings of Liberty to ourselves and our Posterity." Madison argued in the Federalist Papers that "a dependence on the people is no doubt the primary control on the government," explaining that informed citizens are the best way to hold elected officials accountable and restrain government. In 2010, the United States saw a resurgence of citizen activism, notably with the rise of the Tea Party, which made waves in Washington and the states.

Federal spending is at the core of everything that Washington does. That's why a focus on limiting government through spending and tax reform is so important. The same way in which millions of American women are managing their household budgets responsibly, Washington should get control of the federal budget. By enacting firm spending caps, reforming the entitlement programs and taxes, and by controlling the debt, lawmakers can pave the way for higher economic growth and better opportunities for Americans to work, save, invest, and build businesses. Peeling back government in areas better left to the private sector and state and local government, lawmakers can unleash American ingenuity to solve problems and serve the needs of our fellow citizens.

CHAPTER THREE

HEALTH CARE SOLUTIONS FOR ALL AMERICANS

BY HADLEY HEATH MANNING

A very nice nurse named Donna came into the waiting room and told my grandparents and me that mom was almost finished; her biopsy was complete, but she would have to undergo one more mammogram before leaving the hospital that day.

My heart sank for Mom. All that trouble, and still, another painful mammogram. But a few days later, we were thanking God when the results came back—cancer free!

Experiences with our health care system evoke a spectrum of emotions. Stressful situations can require difficult decisions. Sometimes we experience the pain of loss. But on the other hand, health care is also filled with happy stories of healing and new life.

When Americans think about our health care system, they also think of its opaque and complicated payment system. It's frustrating to Americans that we often don't know what the total cost of a procedure or doctor's visit will be. People feel helpless as our premiums and out-of-pocket costs rise, and we often don't know what our alternative options are. Sadly, the ever-rising cost of health care presents a real hurdle to accessing insurance and even health care for millions of people.

Americans want our friends, family and neighbors to get the very best health care at the very best price, but our health care system has been plagued by problems for so long, it's almost as if we can't imagine how great our health care system could be...

- Imagine being able to customize your insurance plan the way you can customize your iPhone.
- Imagine being able to have one continuous insurance policy, even as you change jobs or move across state lines.
- Imagine an insurance policy that doesn't drop you or increase your premiums if you get a bad diagnosis.
- Imagine knowing ahead of time what you will pay for health care services, and how much to expect your insurance policy to pay.
- Imagine being able to compare different doctors or hospitals by quality of care AND price—and choose the one with the best value.
- Imagine YOU in the driver's seat of your health care, instead of being pushed around by insurance companies, big hospitals, or big government.
- Imagine prices going down...instead of up.

All of this can be a reality. We are Americans, after all, and we should lead the world with the best, most efficient and effective health care system.

But we need to understand what's stopping us from achieving this kind of system, and focus on solutions that target the real problems that currently plague our health care system. The trouble is, most people don't understand the strengths and weaknesses of American health care, and don't know the history of our system and how our problems arose.

UNDERSTANDING AMERICA'S STRENGTHS IN THE WORLD OF HEALTH CARE

Sometimes the World Health Organization (WHO) or other agencies will produce international health rankings that suggest that Americans receive worse health care than the rest of the developed world. For example, the United States ranks 42nd in the world for life expectancy (according to the WHO)[1] and 47th for infant mortality (according to the CIA World Fact Book).[2] Rankings like these make Americans feel that our health care system is sub-par in terms of quality and outcomes. But that couldn't be further from the truth.

We should be careful to review international rankings with the best contextual information, and with a fair view of which factors relate to the quality of our health care, and which factors are cultural.

For example, our life expectancy statistics are heavily influenced by high rates of accidental and homicidal deaths in the United States.[3] Also, Americans have higher rates of obesity than other countries, which can shorten life.[4] While all of this is tragic, it doesn't tell us much about our hospitals or how effective they are at saving lives.

Similarly, our infant mortality rate appears to be high, primarily because the U.S. fights hard to save every life, and counts more babies as born alive than other countries do.[5] We also experience a high rate of pregnancy among teenage and obese women, groups that have higher-risk pregnancies, regardless of where they receive health care.[6]

Doctors can advise against unhealthy behaviors—such as smoking, being overweight, or becoming pregnant too young—but lifestyle choices are ultimately left to individuals.

A better measure of our health care system would be how quickly Americans can see a doctor, or how often people survive various illnesses. The WHO ranks the United States #1 in the world for "responsiveness to the needs and choices of the individual patient."[7]

Compared to the rest of the world, Americans do not have to wait long for a doctor's appointment, an important screening, or an elective surgery.[8]

We also have the best cancer survival rates of any country worldwide, which is one reason many of the world's elites travel to the U.S. to be seen in one of our top-notch cancer hospitals.[9]

We also lead the world in medical innovation. A 2009 study showed that American scientists won the Nobel Prize in 33 out of the previous 40 years, whereas scientists from the entire rest of the world won it in only 25 out of those 40 years (often it was shared between Americans and non-Americans).[10] Additionally, of the top 27 drugs and devices, U.S. physicians, companies, and scientists had a hand in developing 20 of them, whereas European physicians, companies and scientists only had a hand in 14.[11]

This means that even the health care that patients are getting in Canada, Europe, Australia, and other places is partly due to the creative capacities of the U.S. health care system. Some of the world's most brilliant minds come to the U.S. to work in researching and developing new drugs and treatments because (among other reasons) the U.S. has intellectual property protections that reward hard work and investment.

The quality of health care in the United States is among the best in the world. We want to keep that in mind as we make changes to our health care system, so that we are careful to preserve our competitive edge in treating serious illnesses and creating new cures.

But our weakness is our bloated, inefficient, and unfair payment system, which can make accessing health care unnecessarily expensive and difficult. To understand the root causes of this problem, we have to study the history of health insurance.

A SHORT HISTORY OF AMERICAN HEALTH CARE AND HEALTH INSURANCE

In the early 1900's, almost no one in the United States carried health insurance or even knew what it was. Health care was simply a transaction between doctors and patients.

Of course, the quality of health care available in those days was nothing compared to today. Medical knowledge advances at break-neck speed, and physicians are constantly trying to put best practices into use.

But we shouldn't confuse the growing prevalence of health insurance with the improving quality of health care available. These two concurrent phenomena had little to do with each other. Health "care" is still something only doctors and health care professionals can deliver. Health "insurance" has become a complex web including carriers, agents, brokers, employers, providers, consumers, and the government.

HEALTH INSURANCE AND THE TAX CODE

During World War II, the federal government imposed price controls that limited employers' ability to increase their workers' wages.[12] Employers found a loophole: They could offer health insurance benefits to attract workers without violating the price control on wage compensation.

A short time later, in 1954, Congress passed a law that exempted health insurance benefits from income taxation.[13] This fueled the fire of employer-sponsored health plans by effectively making this type of health insurance available tax-free, and therefore much more attractive and comparatively less expensive than insurance purchased in the individual market. This continues to be part of our federal tax code today, sixty years later.

State Regulations

Throughout history—anytime previous to the Affordable Care Act of 2010—private health insurance was regulated at the state-level. This means all 50 states made changes to their health insurance markets through state law. It also meant (and continues to mean) that people could not buy health insurance across state lines, where policies might not be compliant with the requirements in the purchasers' state.

Many state governments formed alliances with special interest groups that lobbied for "coverage mandates." For example, a group of acupuncture specialists might approach a politician and ask that their services be mandated for inclusion in every insurance policy sold in the state. Politicians framed these coverage mandates as consumer protections and benefitted along with the special interest groups. But coverage mandates restrict competition and variety in health insurance plans, and force consumers to buy more coverage than they need. Naturally, states with more coverage mandates saw higher premiums, because these mandates raise the costs.[14]

The Great Society

In 1965, the federal government greatly expanded its role in health insurance with the introduction of Medicare (for seniors) and Medicaid (for low-income people). The creators of these government insurance programs promised that they would expand health care access in a cost-effective way. But since that time, both Medicare and Medicaid have developed serious problems.

First, Medicare: Medicare currently insures about 50 million seniors.[15] While these seniors may enjoy the financial benefits of Medicare, funding for this program is in dire straits. The intended funding design was to collect (through payroll taxes) money to use for the health care of seniors when they retired. But in reality, seniors today end up spending about $3 for every $1 they paid into Medicare.[16] This means the program adds greatly to our national debt, and may not be sustainable for future generations.

End-of-life care is some of the most expensive health care there is. Today, many Americans are living far beyond the retirement age of 65. At the same time, there are fewer workers than needed to continue to fund the system (due to reduced fertility and labor force participation rates.) And the imminent retirement of millions more Baby Boomers will come with incredible new costs as well.

Medicaid, too, has been plagued with problems. The government insurance program that currently insures about 66 million low-income people[17] is funded in part by the federal government and in part by states. It takes about 16 percent of the average state budget to provide these health dollars [18](along with federal funding as well).

But even then, the program does not reimburse health care providers very well. In fact, Medicaid only reimburses doctors at about 56 percent of private plan reimbursement.[19] This means health care providers have a strong incentive to see more privately-insured patients, and fewer

Medicaid patients. This makes it harder for Medicaid patients to get the health care they need.

But politicians in Washington have a major obstacle to addressing these problems. Any time anyone tries to make changes to Medicare or Medicaid, he or she is typically accused of taking health care from seniors or low-income people. These serious issues have sadly been reduced to talking points.

The Uninsured

One of the justifications offered for the health reforms of 2010 was the number of people without health insurance. For these uninsured people, accessing and paying for health care services presented a real challenge. Even with a lot of government intervention, many Americans still struggled to get health insurance at all (and sadly, many people will continue to struggle under the Affordable Care Act, which we'll discuss in the next section).

If someone didn't qualify for a government program, but also lacked a job or a health insurance benefit from an employer, then he or she could buy health insurance directly from an insurance carrier in the individual market.

But these plans are only for purchase with after-tax dollars, putting these customers at a disadvantage compared to group (employer-sponsored) plans. Furthermore, before ObamaCare, these policies were risk-rated, meaning it was difficult for older or very sick people to buy new insurance plans. In fact, sometimes people were considered "uninsurable" because they were already diagnosed with serious health problems, and no insurance carriers wanted to sell them a policy.

Inevitably, some of the approximately 50 million uninsured people would occasionally experience a health emergency.[20] Our laws require that any hospital that accepts Medicare (and 99 percent do) must treat any person who is suffering an acute health emergency—regardless of his or her ability to pay. This results in a phenomenon known as "cost-shifting," wherein hospitals charge private insurance companies more to make up for those uninsured people who default on their bills.

So, not only were many Americans concerned with the plight of their uninsured neighbors for humanitarian reasons—they were also concerned because they believed uninsured people contributed to rising costs in health care.

Here are the Cliff Notes on the history of American health care payment and insurance: Prior to 2010, the government controlled one out of every two health care dollars in the United States, making for a hybrid public-private system. But importantly, though elements of our health care system were (and are) *private*, that does not mean we had or have a *free-market* in health care or insurance.

Through state regulation—including coverage mandates—and the federal tax code, the private health insurance market was distorted and the role of insurance companies was inflated. And big federal programs have been increasing their market share and costs since 1965. Nevertheless, many Americans were trapped outside of the insurance system because of too-high costs or a health condition.

2010: THE AFFORDABLE CARE ACT

In 2010, Congress passed and President Barack Obama signed "The Patient Protection and Affordable Care Act," a comprehensive health reform law that has come to be known as "ObamaCare." This legislation touches nearly every part of our health care and health insurance systems.

The main justification for this legislation was the struggle that many Americans faced in obtaining health insurance. As we just discussed, health insurance companies sometimes refused to insure people with pre-existing conditions or offered them prohibitively high prices. The law sought to fix this problem by forcing insurance companies to issue policies to all applicants and to limit how much they could charge.

ObamaCare also had several other aims: It intended to reduce the average cost of health insurance for families and individuals, and to bend the cost curve down in health care services. By regulating insurance companies, changing government programs, and mandating that everyone obtain health insurance, the law's main goal was to increase the number and proportion of Americans with insurance.

Let's look at how the law intended to reach those goals, and how it has been working out in practice.

Regulating Health Insurance

ObamaCare was aimed at reducing cost-shifting in a couple of ways: First, its authors believed that by reducing the number of uninsured people, health providers would not have to reassign defaulted costs to other customers. They sought to attract more insurance customers by regulating the way insurance was sold and by mandating that people buy it.

Second, the law included many regulations on health insurance policies that limited out-of-pocket costs and required coverage for an array of services. This was to ensure that people were no longer "underinsured," or carrying an insurance policy that still left them unable to cover their portion of their bills.

The so-named "Affordable Care Act" included a handful of mechanisms meant to bring down costs for health insurance and health care. Most centrally, it created subsidy and tax credit vehicles (called exchanges), one for each state. Customers with incomes between 100 and 400 percent of the federal poverty line would qualify for some kind of financial help if they purchased insurance in the exchanges.[21]

For people who were older or less healthy, the law attempted to bring down their sky-high insurance costs by requiring that insurance companies offer policies to everyone at more similar prices. The law put in place a one-to-three ratio between the youngest, healthiest customers' prices and the oldest, sickest customers' prices.[22]

The law also doubled down on the role of employers in the U.S. health system, mandating that employers of more than 50 workers provide "adequate" and "affordable" coverage. Employers can be penalized if they ask employees to contribute more than 9.5 percent of their income to a health insurance plan.[23]

Some of these ideas might sound like a good approach, but they create significant problems.

Importantly, subsidies do not reduce costs. They may create the appearance of lower costs to qualifying customers, but this is simply a different form of cost-shifting, from taxpayers to subsidy recipients.

Also, as ObamaCare regulates insurance plans and requires them to be more comprehensive, this inevitably leads to higher average premiums. These premium hikes have been especially stark for young, healthy adults, who, because of the one-to-three ratio (called "age band compression"), are subsidizing the premiums of older, sicker customers.[24]

This means low-risk insurance customers can no longer find premiums that reflect their relatively low utilization of the health care system. Ironically, these high prices discourage low-risk customers from entering insurance pools at all, which undermines ObamaCare's goal of insuring more people.

And finally, as employers are mandated to provide "adequate" insurance coverage (that meets the law's many requirements), this creates a burden and adds to the cost of employing each worker. When the cost of creating a job increases, employers are less likely to create more jobs, which means that there are fewer employees who can participate in employer-plans. Of course, discouraging job creation is also harmful to the overall economy (as was discussed in more detail in chapter one).

Many employers offered health insurance benefits before ObamaCare (due to the tax advantage of employer-sponsored plans discussed earlier), but some did not. Some employers, like retail outlets or fast-food restaurants, offered "mini-med" policies that provided basic—but not comprehensive—health coverage.[25] This mandate presented especially high costs for those employers as they would be forced to expend a much greater share of their companies' resources on health insurance for workers.

Instead of shouldering these enormous costs, some employers have evaded the mandate by moving workers to part-time status. This means employers do not have to provide insurance. But this actually puts workers in a worse situation than before: Before ObamaCare, they may have had a mini-med health policy and worked 40 hours per week. After ObamaCare, they may have no employer-sponsored health coverage and work only 25 hours per week (meaning less take-home pay). This scenario is not uncommon under the new law.[26]

Changing Government Programs

ObamaCare also made significant changes to Medicaid and Medicare.

Medicaid—the government health insurance plan for low-income people—was to be expanded. The original intent of the law was to expand eligibility for the program up to 133 percent of the federal poverty line, meaning more people could take advantage of the "free" government insurance.[27]

But this part of the law ran into constitutional problems. Medicaid is a joint federal-state program, meaning the federal government provides some funding for the program and gives some directives, but the states also fund the program and have the authority to implement it according to state law. Florida and 25 other states challenged the Medicaid expansion at the Supreme Court and won, and as a result Medicaid expansion became optional for states.[28]

Since that decision in summer 2012, 26 states (and the District of Columbia) have decided to expand Medicaid and 24 states have opted out of the expansion.[29]

There are a few reasons some states chose not to expand Medicaid:

About 16 percent of the average state budget is dedicated to Medicaid.[30] Proponents of the expansion point out that for the first few years, the federal government would pay for 90 percent of the costs of the expansion.[31] But states were still concerned about long-term costs, the "woodwork" effect, and state budgets, which must be balanced yearly.

Even if the federal government pays the lion's share of the new costs, all state residents are federal taxpayers too, and some fiscally conservative state leaders were conscious of that and didn't want to add to the country's overall tax and debt burden.

The White House says 3 million people have enrolled in Medicaid since the ObamaCare exchanges opened.[32] Yet not all of those enrollments represent people who are newly eligible; sometimes there is turnover in the Medicaid population, and greater enrollment efforts during an expansion often result in a "woodwork" effect, bringing people out of the woodwork who have always qualified for the program but previously failed to enroll.

And furthermore, as is discussed in more detail in chapter ten, people disagree about whether greater enrollment represents success for a government program. Former President Ronald Reagan would have said, "We should measure welfare's success by how many people leave welfare, not by how many are added."[33]

As discussed earlier, Medicaid faced significant problems before ObamaCare, and the health reform failed to address these problems. The too-low reimbursement rates (about 56 percent compared to commercial plans) mean doctors face a disincentive to accept Medicaid patients.[34]

In fact, a 2011 Health Affairs study shows that 31 percent of primary care doctors aren't taking any new Medicaid patients.[35] The addition of millions of new enrollees exacerbates the shortage of doctors who are available to this population. And multiple other studies suggest that health outcomes for Medicaid patients are much worse than health outcomes for the privately insured.[36] The goal of the Medicaid expansion, of course, was to enroll people who were previously uninsured. But if the expansion mostly moved people from private insurance into Medicaid, this would not only increase public costs, but would result in a lower quality of care for these new Medicaid enrollees.

The health law's changes to *Medicare* (that's the program for seniors) have been much less publicized. The law created a new regulatory body, the "Independent Payment Advisory Board" or IPAB, to reduce per-capita spending in Medicare.[37] This means a board of 15 members are charged with identifying and recommending reductions to the program's budget.

Critics have pointed out that the IPAB would have incredible, perhaps unconstitutional, power. None of the board's members are elected, and they serve six-year terms. In order to block an IPAB recommendation, a *supermajority* in *both houses* of Congress must vote against it *and* agree to an alternative replacement proposal that reduces spending by the same amount.

While IPAB defenders say the health law forbids the Board from rationing health care services to seniors, others recognize that by reducing payments to Medicare doctors for certain services, the result could be back-door rationing, or disincentives for doctors to offer certain treatments. This is what led Sarah Palin to famously decry the IPAB as a "death panel."[38]

Republicans have also recommended slowing the rate of growth in the Medicare program. Most notably, 2012 Vice Presidential candidate and House Budget Chairman Paul Ryan has proposed several budgets that would restrain Medicare growth according to a formula that is very similar to the formula used by the IPAB.[39]

The important difference, of course, is in the approach: The IPAB would cut reimbursements to doctors, and Paul Ryan's plans would transition Medicare into a "defined contribution" or "premium support" program. This means individual Medicare patients—not a government board—would decide how to use their allotted health care dollars. (You can read more about this idea at the end of this chapter.)

Mandating Health Insurance

Finally, one of ObamaCare's most central provisions is the individual mandate to obtain health insurance. If Americans fail to obtain insurance (and do not qualify for a exemption), they must pay a fine. This provision has by far been the most unpopular piece of ObamaCare, but it remains law.[40]

From a public policy standpoint, the individual mandate is necessary to the ObamaCare approach. The regulations on health insurance favor high-risk (sicklier) customers and disadvantage low-risk (healthier) customers, which could incentivize healthy people to leave insurance pools. In order to avoid this, the mandate attempts to change consumers' cost-benefit analysis and the incentive structure in the law to encourage more to purchase insurance.

Florida, 25 other states, and the National Federation of Independent Businesses (a small business group) also challenged the individual mandate at the Supreme Court. In 2012, the Court upheld the mandate penalty as an exercise of Congress's taxing power.[41]

The individual mandate has critics on the Right and the Left. Both see the government requirement to purchase a private good from a private company as an unfair intrusion into free association. For one thing, it burdens customers who would prefer not to buy the product. For another, it amounts to cronyism. The government is essentially showing favor to one private industry (health insurance) by requiring that everyone buy its products. Imagine if your family ran a Christmas tree farm, and the government required everyone to buy a Christmas tree. This would be great for business!

Not only does the individual mandate mean that Americans must obtain health insurance, but it also means everyone has to have insurance that is *compliant*, or covers the "Essential Health Benefits" as defined by the Department of Health and Human Services.[42] Even customers who were privately insured before ObamaCare are finding that their old health plans did not meet the law's requirements. That's why, contrary to the promises of many politicians, millions of private insurance customers have had their pre-ObamaCare insurance plans cancelled.[43]

The "Essential Health Benefits," or EHBs, function at the federal level much like state-level coverage mandates before ObamaCare. While the government passes them off as consumer protections, they are actually just limitations on the variety of insurance plans offered in the market. They also raise the cost of the most basic insurance plans. (It's like requiring that all pizzas come with a certain number and type of toppings. Plain cheese, the cheapest option, is no longer allowed on the menu.)

When government starts dictating what's in every insurance plan, we start running into other market distortions. For example, among the EHBs are all FDA-approved contraceptive methods, and these contraceptives must be covered at the *first-dollar*. ObamaCare supporters say this represents progress for women, because it means women will no longer pay any co-pay for birth controls, emergency contraception, or even sterilizations.

But the mandate to include this coverage doesn't actually save money. It simply hides the cost of contraception by rolling it into higher premiums. In fact, it may ultimately contribute to *higher* costs in contraceptives, because it removes any price competition from the sight of consumers.[44]

This mandate has created other conflicts. Employer-sponsored plans must also cover all EHBs, including the full gamut of contraceptives. Some religious employers object to this because they consider some or all of the forms of contraception morally wrong.[45] They don't want to spend their resources this way, and they shouldn't be mandated to do so. The United States has always been a beacon of religious freedom, and people of all beliefs should be free to live and do business in accordance with their conscience.

Mandates on individuals and employers create a mess of problems. Surely there is a better way to solve our country's health care problems.

Instead of a mandate-based approach, some progressives support moving to a "single-payer" health care system, where private insurance companies no longer exist, and the government serves as the only payer for all medical expenses for all citizens. Health care would all be funded by tax dollars. In the past, this has been called "socialized medicine," but the latest re-branding of government-run health care is called "single-payer."

Conservatives and libertarians on the other hand, see both a mandate-centric and a government-centric health system as harmful to individual freedom, market competition in health care, and therefore health care quality. Free-market advocates have other health reform ideas, which you can read about in the pages ahead.

THE HEART OF THE DEBATE

At the heart of our nation's debate about health reform is this question: Are the problems in our health system due to private markets or government intervention? Because we've had a hybrid public-private system in the past, and because ObamaCare continues on this path (increasing the role of government, but maintaining private ownership of insurance companies), the debate continues.

Those on the Left want to point to what they consider to be inequalities and uncertainties in a private-sector approach. Those on the Right emphasize the way government intervention in health care restricts choices and encourages inefficiency.

While the United States may have a part-*public*, part-*private* health system, what we do not have is a *free-market* health system that is centered on the individual patient, and driven by the choices of the individual consumer. Even though much of our health system remains privately owned, under ObamaCare, this ownership is a facade. The government makes the real decisions, telling insurers what kind of policies to sell to whom and when and at what price... and telling consumers they must comply.

People will debate whether ObamaCare was passed with good intentions. Even if we presume that it was, the law can't be judged on its intentions. It must be judged on its results. The fact remains that the law did not fix the real problems that existed in the American health care system, and it's time to consider other ways to transition our health care system into something stronger, better, and freer for everyone.

It has been a real challenge for free-market supporters to paint a picture of their ideal health system because it would be very unlike the current American system, and no other country in the world provides a good example. But like the exercise at the beginning of the chapter, we have to imagine how great our health care system could be if competition were vibrant and consumers were empowered.

FREE-MARKET, PATIENT-CENTERED, CONSUMER-DRIVEN HEALTH CARE

How do we get there? Too often proponents of ObamaCare have misrepresented their ideological opponents, saying that conservatives have no ideas when it comes to health reform. This creates a false choice for the American people: Support ObamaCare or support the status quo ante.

In reality, there have been dozens of conservative health reform plans offered.[46] Some are the products of think tanks or other non-profit organizations; some are pieces of legislation sponsored by Members of Congress. All of them have a few principles in common: They seek to put consumers and patients at the center of the health care system. They force insurance companies to compete with each other, resulting in better prices, greater choice, and higher quality in health insurance plans. And they uphold the basic American principles of responsibility, fairness, and care for the destitute.

Choice, Portability, and Affordability

Americans shouldn't have to worry about losing their insurance coverage when they change jobs. But, as discussed previously, the link between employment and insurance makes it difficult for people to maintain continuous, portable coverage, and it makes health insurance markets less competitive.

Congress should start by equalizing the tax treatment of employer and individual insurance, through a cap or elimination of the tax exemption of employer-sponsored plans, coupled with either a universal tax credit or deduction for individually- (or family) purchased plans.

This would make health insurance more affordable for people outside of the employer-sponsored (group) market, and would allow people who are currently in a group plan to apply their tax credit or deduction toward their current plan, or a different plan if that's their choice. Ultimately, the goal is not to take away the freedom of people to offer or buy employer-centric insurance, but to level the playing field for group and non-group plans.

Another restriction that currently limits competition among health insurance companies (and limits the choices of consumers) is that Americans are only allowed to purchase plans offered by insurance carriers within their state of residence. Instead, Americans should be able to buy insurance across state lines. This would open up what are currently 50 different tightly regulated markets into one nationwide market where the best-fit insurance plans in the country are available to everyone, regardless of where we live. Removing this restriction would also mean that no one would have to change insurance simply because he or she moved from one state to another.

The goal is to allow the creation of a true market that offers more choices, improved portability, and affordability.

Fiscal Responsibility

In our current public-private hybrid system, the U.S. government already spends more than $4,000 per year per person on health care (through a complex maze of entitlements and subsidies).[47] This is more than most other OECD countries, even countries with socialized health care and little private expenditures. Health care represents a growing share of our national economy—approaching 20 percent—and much of this is due to growing public expenditures.[48]

Health policy desperately needs a dose of fiscal responsibility. A wide-reaching tax deduction or credit for the purchase of health insurance would reduce revenues, but would also replace many of the current layers of spending and subsidies. Also, the present limitless tax advantage enjoyed by employer-sponsored insurance should be capped or eliminated. The goal should be equal tax treatment of employer-sponsored and individual insurance, along with a net reduction in taxation and spending.

Caring for People in Need

Before ObamaCare, Americans were rightly concerned about the plight of people with pre-existing health conditions who struggled to obtain and maintain coverage. High health costs across the board also met low-income people with an affordability hurdle.

The problem of pre-existing conditions is perhaps the hardest problem America faces when it comes to health policy and reform. But there are various ways we can address pre-existing conditions without ObamaCare-style mandates on insurers and consumers.

In the long run, many conservatives and champions of the free-market would like to see the private sector innovate a solution to this problem. One such innovative idea is called "health status" or "guaranteed renewable" insurance. This is basically a rider to your health insurance coverage that would protect you (as a healthy person) from the threat of a steep premium increase (or a policy cancellation) if you were one day diagnosed with a health condition. This encourages people to buy and maintain continuous health insurance when they are healthy, and allows them to keep that coverage at an affordable rate, even if they become very sick.

Insurance companies will never be free to innovate with these different types of coverage options so long as they are as tightly regulated as they are today.

Furthermore, for people with pre-existing conditions, *states* are already free to create and manage high-risk pools. Essentially, a high-risk pool groups together people who, because of a health condition, cannot find affordable health coverage in the private market. Then, the state subsidizes the insurance of this group, focusing assistance on people who truly need it (as opposed to ObamaCare-style subsidies, available to even healthy people at some incomes).

ObamaCare established a federal high risk pool program that turned out to be an utter failure: The program required applicants to go uninsured six months before qualifying, and even then ran out of money far too early, necessitating a suspension in enrollment and leaving thousands without coverage.[49]

High-risk pools should be the prerogative and purview of states. Safety nets are better administered at the local level, where leaders know better the needs of their state's population.

The same principle should be applied to Medicaid. Rather than expansion, this program needs reform. Medicaid should be block granted to the states, which should be free to determine eligibility levels and benefits. Some pilot programs have already seen success by introducing consumer choice to the Medicaid program and allowing beneficiaries to choose among private plans, where they are better served. This approach not only saves states money, but also results in better health care, outcomes, and satisfaction levels for enrollees.[50]

This approach—where beneficiaries have a fixed amount of money to use toward a private plan of their choice—is called a "premium support" model. Rep. Paul Ryan has suggested that we transition the Medicare program to this more competitive model as well, so that Medicare patients can have better insurance, and so that funding for the program can become more sustainable.[51] Infusing market competition into government programs has been proven successful before, as we've seen in Medicare Part D.[52]

Finally, we should never forget to emphasize the important role that free and charitable clinics play in our health care system to help provide for those in need. Many doctors and health care professionals want to dedicate part of their time to charitable work, and we should make it easy for them to do so. Many citizens want to financially support charitable clinics in their communities, and churches and other charities often help people in their communities who face extraordinarily challenging medical bills.

Government doesn't have to be the solution to every problem; the "social safety net" should start in civil society, where we can care for our neighbors and friends through voluntary relationships.

Preserving America's Strengths in Health Care

Whatever the specifics of a free-market health plan, legislators should keep in mind the areas where America leads. As discussed earlier, the rest of the world depends on us to practice quality, individual-focused medicine, and to develop tomorrow's treatments and cures. In order to continue to attract and retain the world's best physicians, we should protect their autonomy. Medical malpractice insurance and the threat of lawsuits add to the cost of practicing medicine. College, medical school, and residency training also present a great investment, and doctors should be able to pay off their debts. This means we need reform in higher education (getting the government out of student lending) and also need to reform how physicians are reimbursed in Medicare and Medicaid.

Similarly, innovators in the health care space should be able to recoup investments in the research and development of new treatments and drugs. Reasonable protections for their intellectual property should be respected in the United States and abroad.

THE BIG PICTURE FOR HEALTH REFORM

We are in the midst of a very important debate about health care in our country. Do we need more government control, or less?

Health care is such a deeply personal aspect of life. Every individual has her own body, her own preferences, her own beliefs, and her own health care needs. It follows that the government's role in these personal issues should be limited. There is no one-size-fits-all health care system or health insurance plan. While government (at both the state and federal level) played too big a role before ObamaCare, the new law has taken us in the wrong direction, adding even more regulations, taxes, subsidies, and market distortions to the mix.

Instead, our health policies should seek to foster a vibrant marketplace where providers, patients, insurers, hospitals, innovators, and manufacturers are free to work together toward more cures, longer, healthier lives, and a higher quality of life for all. This approach provides the maximum amount of choice to consumers and patients—and would unleash the great capability of the American people to freely work together in our marketplaces and our communities toward fuller, healthier lives.

CHAPTER FOUR

WOMEN AT WORK

BY SABRINA SCHAEFFER

S ometimes I wonder about my choices.

My work-life situation means I'm frequently frazzled, trying to direct a staff call from my car on the way to a school performance, or rushing from a meeting to pick the kids up from a birthday party.

But then again, I'm pretty happy with my situation. I married relatively young (for this generation) and now have three wonderful children. I have the opportunity to work full-time from home, so I can see my youngest when he gets up from a nap or my girls when they come home from school. And I have a fair amount of flexibility, so on days when I'm shooting off emails by 6:30 am, I have the freedom to take my girls to swim practice in the afternoon.

One Saturday morning stands out in particular, when I agreed to an early morning TV interview. I woke up at the crack of dawn while the family was all still asleep and dragged myself to the studio. But what made it all worthwhile was meeting everyone afterward at the local diner for breakfast. It was a moment of work-life balance bliss. A little tired perhaps, but grateful for the momentary chance to "have it all."

I'll admit there are many days when life feels more frightful than delightful. The work-life juggle can wear out even the most organized of working parents. And there's certainly a financial tradeoff for the kind of flexibility my family and I enjoy. I could have pursued career paths where my remuneration would have been higher, but my hours in an office would have been fixed and long. Bigger companies would have likely offered me even greater job security, but it's unlikely I could work full-time from my home office.

I'm among the fortunate women whose education and experience affords such options. Many women have a tough time finding a job to pay the bills, much less one that offers personal satisfaction and a work-life balance. Yet it turns out that what I want isn't so different from what the vast majority of working mothers want: flexibility. A recent Pew Social Trends report found that 70 percent of working mothers—compared to only 46 percent of working fathers—regard flexibility as more important than higher pay. Similarly, only 23 percent of working mothers said they would choose to work full-time if they had the option.[1]

Sometimes it seems like the conversation about women and work focuses almost exclusively on salary—how to help working women earn more money. But as Claire Shipman and Katty Kay wrote in their book *Womenomics*, "Winning your professional liberation does demand a rethink—a fundamental reevaluation of what success really means."[2]

Certainly for myself—and for many women—success is defined by doing something that is personally rewarding. And for me that means both in the office and at home.

Many women share my priorities. In fact, a 2009 study conducted by the Federal Reserve Bank of New York considered what factors male and female students use to choose their college major. While it's hard to pinpoint just one reason for their decisions, and both sexes weighed potential outcomes, women generally placed more emphasis on finding rewarding work, while men were more inclined to seek out opportunities to improve their social status and increase their salary.[3]

The reality is no one, man or woman, can do "all things at once," to borrow a phrase from TV host and author Mika Brezinkski[4]. No conversation about women at work can ignore that there are still only 24 hours in a day, and both men and women have to make choices as to how to allocate their time.

My circumstance—like *all* work-life situations—has its challenges, because no choices are without a downside. I've missed field trips because I have work, and I've skipped out of a work responsibility because of a school play. And, like everyone, I often get things wrong.

The big difference is that I was fortunate enough to be able to make the *good* choices in life. Should I go to this school or the better school? Should we have children now or later? Should I stay home full-time or part-time?

The purpose of this chapter is to figure out how *more* women can have an opportunity to make such choices that reflect their own values and preferences. Life will always be filled with challenges and tradeoffs, but our goal should be to ensure that more women have the freedom to make the choices that make sense for them and their families.

This chapter will tell the story of women at work today. It will explore how the workplace has changed in recent decades and how women are the impetus driving that change. It will push back on some of the myths that still exist about the "wage gap" and pervasive gender discrimination; but it will also acknowledge the very real challenges that persist, especially for women at the lower end of the socio-economic scale. And it will offer an *alternative* solution driven by individuals, our communities, and the private sector to improve the workplace for women—not just give them more opportunities to sue employers—without more government intervention.

WORKPLACE LANDSCAPE

Putting aside the challenges of balancing work with motherhood, it's good to step back and look at all the ways women are helping shape and transform the American workforce and workplace in a positive way.

Today, women make up 47 percent of the workforce and are increasingly valuable to businesses.[5] It's not surprising why: Women today receive 57 percent of bachelor's degrees, 59 percent of master's degrees, and more than half of PhDs.[6]

And women are not simply participating at higher numbers, but filling jobs that require more education and greater skills. In fact, the largest group of working women—33 percent—are those with college degrees. Forty percent of privately-held businesses are owned by women.[7]

This all adds up to women having a lot of economic power. Even back in 2001, Catalyst found that together women earned $2 trillion.[8] That's a whole lot of money to allocate, and, in fact, women are the leading consumers of everything from groceries to electronics to cars.[9] According to the media and consumer research firm GfK MRI, just shy of 75 percent of women identify themselves as the primary shopper in their household.[10]

Again Kay and Shipman note that, "In the United States nearly half of all shareholders are women, half of all computers are bought by women, and women are responsible for 83 percent of all consumer purchases."[11] Bottom line, businesses view women as critical members of their teams not only because of the skills they bring to the job, but also as essential customers.

Traditional feminists often lament the shortage of women in top leadership positions, but the fact is the number of women in senior management positions has been rising sharply.[12] And today there's a growing list of female business leaders who are household names: Facebook's COO Sheryl Sandberg, Yahoo's Marissa Mayer, IBM's Virginia Rometty, GM's Mary Barra, Hewlett-Packard's Meg Whitman and former CEO Carly Fiorina, to name a few.

Even in industries like technology, which are often perceived as dominated by men, we're seeing a host of women rise to executive positions. A recent article in *The Washington Post* acknowledged that while women may be less noticeable than men in the technology industry, women are flooding the field, often working outside the highly visible Silicon Valley.[13]

What's more, shifting cultural norms and changes in technology have revolutionized the American workplace. It's hard to forget, for instance, the uproar that occurred when Yahoo's CEO Marissa Mayer issued a company-wide ban on telecommuting. It wasn't just Yahoo employees who were upset. It was a much larger reaction from millions of Americans who have benefited from telecommuting and the modern American workplace.

As is discussed in chapter nine, somewhere between 20-30 million people work from home at least one day a month.[14] An estimated 3.1 million Americans (not including those who are self-employed) work from home full time—about 2.5 percent of Americans. And even during the economic downturn of recent years, telecommuting grew by 11.4 percent from 2008 to 2011.[15] Working mothers may have been the impetus for increased telecommuting and other kinds of "nontraditional benefits" like job sharing and a compressed workweek, but these workplace transformations have helped employees at all levels of the pay scale, and have been a huge victory for anyone like myself who wants that coveted flexibility.

Still, despite what I view as an overall positive picture for women today, I'm not Pollyanna-ish about the challenges that face many women, especially those with less education and fewer opportunities. There are plenty of women, especially unmarried mothers, facing hardship during this current economic downturn.

The number of single-parent households, where women are often the sole breadwinner, has risen dramatically in recent decades. In 1960 the majority of single-mothers were divorced, separated, or widowed—only 4 percent were actually never married—but today the picture looks very different. Today 44 percent of single mothers have never been married. And most of these single-parent households are headed by under-educated, over-worked mothers with little flexibility whose earning potential is far below their married peers, averaging only $23,000 a year.[16]

A separate study on Millennials by the Pew Research Center also focuses on the decline in marriage. Not surprisingly this trend is leading to an uptick in out-of-wedlock births: "47 percent of births to women in the Millennial generation were non-marital, compared with 21 percent among older women."[17] But this shift away from marriage is leaving serious economic consequences in its wake.

Too many of these women lack any choices, let alone good choices. The workplace is no longer viewed as a place of opportunity so much as a way to simply make ends meet. But the hardships that many women face can't be solved through a one-size-fits all piece of "workplace legislation," the way so many progressives suggest. In fact, most proposals offered by feminists on the left and their Democratic allies would be counterproductive, giving women less choice and flexibility in the workplace. Truly helping these women begins with education reform and extends to broad economic reform to spur economic growth and job creation.

WHY THE WAGE GAP?

At the heart of the "War on Women" rhetoric that started in 2010 and escalated in 2012 is the "wage gap" statistic that women only earn 77 cents for every dollar a man earns.

The statistic is repeated so frequently that it has likely become as familiar as the Pledge of Allegiance to most Americans. A basic search on the White House website for the phrase "wage gap" brings up over 33,000 results: speeches, press releases, articles, infographics. Within Democratic circles, telling Americans that women are paid less than men is like saying the sky is blue. And it's repeated practically as often as the morning weather report.

The problem, of course, is that the 77-cent statistic is grossly misleading. The number comes from the Department of Labor, and it compares the median wages of a full-time working man with a full-time working woman. But this is a comparison of averages and is like comparing apples to oranges. The statistic doesn't take into account the number of hours worked, the profession, the job responsibilities, or the educational or professional experience of the workers, for instance. Even without controlling for many of these different variables, the newer number from the Department of Labor is 81 cents—but you'll rarely hear a Democrat even say that.[18]

More importantly, if you control for those factors, economists find that just a very small portion of wage gap remains unexplained. One such economist is June O'Neill at the City University of New York, who studied data from 2000 and found that after controlling for factors such as college major, work experience, career choice, and time spent out of the workforce, a meager 3.3 percent wage gap remained.[19]

Government studies have revealed similar findings. Diana Furchgott-Roth (a contributor to this book) points to several studies in her book *Women's Figures*. In 2009 the Department of Labor commissioned a project by CONSAD Research, which found women make 94 percent of what their male counterparts earn.[20]

And even progressive women's groups have found as much (though they'll be loathe to admit it). Just two weeks before the 2012 presidential election, The American Association of University Women released a study, Graduating with a Pay Gap, which tried to stress a pay disparity, even while its own research found the wage gap to be about 6.6 cents after controlling for relevant factors.

So the more important question is *why does that small pay gap remain*? As women are increasingly outpacing men educationally and professionally, it simply doesn't comport that the wage gap is entirely a function of broad based gender bias.

We know that women's choices—from their college major to time spent out of the workplace to hours spent in the office each day—impact their salaries. Some of our choices may be explained by biology and may reflect innate aptitudes and preferences, while others may be a function of societal norms and culture. Of course, nature and nurture can be difficult to separate and individuals with a natural talent may find they are more driven in an environment that makes use of that capability. What's more, we know that women negotiate their salaries far less frequently than men do.

Generally, however, it's clear that the primary driver of the wage gap is that more women choose to take time out of the workplace to raise a family. As the Manhattan Institute's Kay Hymowitz writes, "The main reason that women spend less time at work than men—and that women are unlikely to be the richer sex—is obvious: children."[21]

And it does seem pretty clear. As *Time Magazine* reported just last year, unmarried women in their twenties were making significantly more than their male counterparts.[22] Flash-forward five or ten years when the same women have decided to start families and take time out of the workplace, and that pendulum begins to shift in the other direction, with men out-earning women.

Liberal feminists and Democrats too often point to this pay gap as a sign of persistent discrimination, a society that is hostile toward women and as evidence of the need for greater government oversight. But the reality is women in America today have more choices than ever before, and the gap results from them exercising those choices.

WHY WE CARE SO MUCH ABOUT THE WAGE GAP – AND WHAT THE OTHER SIDE PROPOSES TO "SOLVE" THE PROBLEM

Why is this conversation about the wage gap so important? At its core the faulty wage gap statistic perpetuates the myth that society and the workplace are inherently antagonistic toward women. Taken a step further, it frames women as a victim class in need of special protections from government. And these "protections" would not only grow government unnecessarily, but also backfire on women, making them more costly to employ.

The grossly inflated 77-cent statistic is used to justify passing or expanding a range of workplace regulations, including laws like the Lilly Ledbetter Fair Pay Act and the Family and Medical Leave Act, as well as proposed laws like the Paycheck Fairness Act and the FAMILY Act. All of these policies may be grounded in good intentions, but have serious economic consequences for both men and women. The cost of protective legislation is high. The Obama administration and women's groups on the left tout the Lilly Ledbetter Fair Pay Act as a great accomplishment for women. But the Lilly Ledbetter Act doesn't actually create equal pay; nor does it protect women against gender-based discrimination. It simply extends the 180-day statue of limitations for filing an equal-pay discrimination suit established under Title VII of the 1964 Civil Rights

Act, stating that the 180 days resets with every new paycheck. What this means is that an employee who feels she was discriminated against, but doesn't come forth at the time, can wait 5, 10 years—or in the case of Lilly Ledbetter two decades—before filing suit.

Certainly it's possible that an employee may not come forth within the first 180 days of being subject to discrimination. But we already have longer time limits for suing in place through the Equal Pay Act, which has a three-year deadline for willful discrimination claims and a two-year deadline for all other claims of sex-based or race-based discrimination in pay. And certainly there is a need for some limits to a company's liability for personnel decisions made by one set of managers. An open-ended time horizon means that companies can face litigation for events that took place years after all the relevant management officers have left, making justice impossible.

Proposed laws like the Paycheck Fairness Act (PFA) are equally ineffective at closing the pay gap and are poised to have a negative economic impact on women in the workplace.[23] Although sold as necessary to "close the wage gap," the PFA again centers solely on making lawsuits against employers more profitable, which has dubious benefits for individual workers, but great appeal to trail lawyers.

For example, if passed, the PFA would limit the reasons employers could give for salary differences among workers. This would make it easier for employees to file suits, but would also make the workplace less flexible and make it nearly impossible for employers to tie compensation to work quality. As I discussed earlier in this chapter, often women would choose flexibility over salary. Many women would gladly take a lower salary if it means they can leave the office at 3 pm, or only work four days a week. But a law like the PFA would limit the ability for an employee to freely negotiate with her employer and ultimately make the workplace more rigid.

While progressives talk about this bill as "common sense" legislation, and it's framed in terms of "protecting" women, they overlook the fact that women—and their families—benefit tremendously from the flexible work environment that these regulations threaten.

Similarly, the proposed FAMILY Act in the Senate would dramatically refashion and expand the existing Family and Medical Leave Act to provide, in effect, a new paid leave federal entitlement program. If passed, the FAMILY Act would automatically entitle workers to sixty days of family and medical leave during which they would be guaranteed two-thirds of their average pay, with no consideration for the fact that most Americans already have access to leave or for the unintended consequences of such a law.

As with the PFA, proponents of the law insist that the FAMILY Act would provide necessary leave time to workers, especially new mothers. But also like the PFA, the FAMILY Act is the enemy of flexibility and workplace opportunity for women. Once again advocates focus solely on the "benefits"—money flowing to those newly eligible for paid leave time— but ignore the considerable costs.

Not only would this program require its own dedicated payroll tax, and likely encourage many private companies to do away with existing leave policies, but it would also encourage businesses to avoid hiring women (particularly of childbearing age). Businesses would have good reason to assume that such women are likely to take leave for several months' time, with no ability to negotiate partial-work arrangements that benefit both worker and employer. In the long run, women would become costlier and more difficult to employ. The result would be fewer opportunities— particularly leadership opportunities—as a result.[24]

The bottom line is that men and women are already protected against baseless gender discrimination under the 1963 Equal Pay Act and the 1964 Civil Rights Act. These laws already state that it's illegal for an employer not to hire someone or to compensate someone differently because of his or her gender. Companies are also increasingly offering more generous benefits and finding new work arrangements that help women balance work and family life, because they see women as valuable employees.

Moving forward, this is the logic we should be encouraging, rather than government mandates that make women more expensive, and less attractive, potential employees. The common denominator with all these protective laws is that they advance the idea that the workplace is hostile to women, pit women and men against each other, and ultimately won't create equal pay or advance women's economic prospects. Instead they'll benefit trial lawyers, please feminist activists, and boost votes for Democrats.

ALTERNATIVE SOLUTIONS TO IMPROVING THE WORKPLACE

Every year publications like *Fortune, Working Mother* and others release lists of the best companies for working women.[25] These lists generally identify businesses that have the most family-friendly policies and flexible work environments for their employees, but some also focus on businesses with women in positions of leadership.

These lists include the majority of household name companies from Blue Cross Blue Shield—which is recognized for providing $4,000 annual tuition aid packages for employees in school, flexible schedules, lengthy paid maternity and paternity leaves, as well as mom-focused classes in prenatal yoga and baby CPR—to Verizon Communications, which began its Mobility at Work program in 2012 to make office space available to the growing number of employees who are not tied to a specific location. Seventy-six percent of Verizon's workforce already telecommutes.[26]

The reality is that the workplace is changing—quickly and for the better. Providing sensible leave policies, tuition aid, day care backups, and generous benefit packages has become increasingly expected and necessary to attract and retain top professionals. And these policies trickle down. Wal-Mart is one such company that initially started a flexible work policy in its legal department, in which there were no official set hours. Not surprisingly other departments caught wind of this innovation, and the company began working to implement the program more broadly.[27]

And where businesses may still lag behind, there is a robust private industry devoted to helping women achieve higher pay. Sheryl Sandberg was not the first woman to write the "rules for success." If you look up Sandberg's book *Lean In* on Amazon, you'll find an additional 17 pages of similar books that teach women how to negotiate, how to speak up, and how to make sure they position themselves to get the corner office.

And if books aren't enough, a host of organizations like 85 Broads, Negotiating Women, She Negotiates, and C4CM (Center for Competitive Management), have emerged to help women maximize their success in the workplace. Conferences, networking events, corporate training, training courses, video seminars—these organizations are focused on giving women the tools to handle conflict, overcome risk aversion, build alliances, and learn to negotiate. In short, there is an entire industry devoted to helping women overcome remaining hurdles in the workplace.

Ultimately I suspect many of these problems will continue to diminish as women continue to excel, and the workforce naturally adapts to their needs and demands. In the end, however, the best solution for a woman who is being paid unfairly or who is unhappy in her place of employment is a strong economy with healthy job growth, so that women can look for another employer and have a greater range of employment opportunities.

Government can make it easier for women (and men) by encouraging job creation and reducing the burdens they place on parents. Rather than new mandates and costly government programs—which tend to reward one set of choices (such as working) over another—policymakers should seek to consolidate programs geared to helping parents and returning those resources to parents in the form of lower tax payments across the board. Ensuring that there is a robust job market and increasing families' take-home pay can help give more women (and men) the ability to make the choices about how best to balance their career, family, and other life goals.

CONCLUSION

When Sheryl Sandberg came out with her best-selling book *Lean In* last year, she reignited the fiery debate over women's participation in the workplace. It was just the latest in the perpetual conversation about women at work and work-life balance that is punctuated every so often by an inflammatory statement or article about women "having it all."

These episodes usually explode into hot debates over gender equality, gender differences, and workplace fairness. And too often the outcome is a renewed push by the progressive women's lobby for greater government intervention, with little consideration to the real need for or unintended consequences of bigger, more intrusive government.

Women today have been granted great liberties, tremendous opportunities, and, in some respects, new challenges. Any working mother is familiar with the balancing act as they rush off to a job outside the home, while maintaining the normal responsibilities of keeping a home and raising a family. Some women will choose a high-powered career on Wall Street. Others will stay at home to raise their family. And most of us will create something in the middle—a work-life tapestry designed to suit our personal needs, which will likely change and take on different forms over the years.

This is all by way of recognizing that the workplace—nor the home—is perfect, and there are still changes that can be made at the individual and societal level to improve the lives of women and their families.

Still, overall, women today have an unprecedented opportunity to succeed in their careers and to design a lifestyle that suits their needs and wants, and those of their families. And that's something to be recognized and protected. This great opportunity women have today to find a balance between home and work is delicate and can easily be overturned by an overly ambitious state that seeks to try to legislate "perfection."

CHAPTER FIVE

EXPANDING EDUCATION FREEDOM, K-12 AND HIGHER EDUCATION

BY VICKI E. ALGER

Americans increasingly expect to be able to tailor their lives according to their unique needs and preferences. Employment practices are becoming more flexible as a growing number of Americans telecommute and use new technologies to work at odd hours and from remote locations. Americans pick and choose their entertainment at the time of their convenience.

There is no reason that the same cannot be true in the education sector. Americans should be able to choose from a wide variety of education providers, from schools to job training programs, educational games and virtual learning opportunities, that serve people of all ages.

And in fact, there are more educational services available to more students than ever before. A growing number of educational choice programs throughout the country are providing parents the schooling options they think are best for their children—regardless or their income or address. Decades' worth of evidence now shows that parental choice programs are constitutional, cost-effective, and best of all, they work.

Yet sadly, too much of the formal American education system ignores the availability of such services and the benefits of such flexibility and specialization. Instead they are moving in the opposite direction toward one-size-fits-all schooling, thanks in no small part to a growing number of federal initiatives that were supposed to improve achievement, especially among disadvantaged students.

Providing students with a solid elementary and secondary foundation is critical for students to succeed in college and in life. Yet there is growing concern that a college education is beyond the financial reach of too many young people and their families. What's more, evidence is mounting that students are more likely to leave college with crushing debt instead of job prospects—in spite of expensive federal programs designed to keep college affordable and accessible.

For all the noble intentions animating federal programs that seek to improve the learning opportunities of Americans of all ages, these government policies have become an obstacle to parents and young adults choosing the options they think are best. This chapter takes a closer look at how expanding educational options at all levels is working for schoolchildren, their parents, and young people working toward college degrees.

Americans deserve the world's best education system, one that allows learning opportunities for people of any age. The good news is that commonsense reforms to our education system can make this possible, by returning control of resources to education consumers and encouraging competition and innovation by education providers.

A NATIONAL SNAPSHOT K-12 SCHOOLING OPTIONS

Most American schoolchildren attend assigned public schools based on where their families can afford to live; however, in the past 20 years the proportion of students attending assigned public schools has dropped to 73 percent down from 80 percent.[1]

It's a tremendously positive trend that a growing number of parents are actively selecting their child's school, since research consistently shows that simply letting parents pick their children's public schools instead of assigning students to a school based solely on location can have a dramatic impact on school performance. Schools risk losing students and their associated funding to other schools if they fail to provide a positive educational experience. As one distinguished education economist put it, public school choice "is the most powerful market force in American public education," capable of improving school productivity up to 28 percent.[2]

Other research finds that the competitive pressure to perform when parents are empowered to pick their children's schools yields improvements in student math achievement comparable to increasing funding by nearly $3,400 per pupil.[3] Giving parents more freedom to choose their children's schools also produces the same math gains as raising families' annual median household incomes more than $8,700.[4] In fact, compared to areas where children simply attend assigned public schools, in areas where parents pick their children's public schools math achievement averages 3 national percentile points higher, reading achievement averages 4 to 6 national percentile points higher, and spending averages 8 percent *lower* because schools that compete for students get more bang for every education buck.[5]

Today, parents of school-age children make use of a variety of alternative school options, including:

Charter Schools

Charter schools are independently-operated public schools that must abide by the same admissions, testing, and accountability mandates as traditional district-run public schools. They typically receive around 80 percent of the funding traditional public schools receive (around 72 percent for urban charter schools),[6] and do not have taxing authority. Charter schools must meet all the goals defined in their charter contract or be shut down. In exchange for lower funding, charter schools have greater flexibility over their curriculum.[7] Currently, more than 2.5 million students are attending nearly 6,500 charter schools in 40 states and the District of Columbia.[8]

In addition to giving parents more options, charter schools are also powerful reform vehicles. Back in 2010, for example, California became the first state to enact Parent Trigger legislation. Under this law, parents with children in chronically failing public schools no longer need to wait years—even decades—for bureaucratic and politicized improvement processes to take effect. After gathering enough signatures from parents and teachers, parents can submit a petition to the state education agency to have the school converted to a locally managed charter school instead of a district-run school. Today six more states have enacted similar legislation: Connecticut, Indiana, Louisiana, Mississippi, Ohio (pilot program in the Columbus School District), and Texas. Another 25 states have considered enacting Parent Trigger laws as well.[9]

Homeschooling

While laws vary from state to state, in many places parents can design their own curricula, choose the nationally standardized tests their children will take, and guide their children to learn at their own pace. As many as 2 million students are homeschooled, and research has consistently shown that across core subjects such as reading, math, and social studies, homeschooled students typically score close to the 90th percentile on nationally standardized tests regardless of their families' socioeconomic backgrounds, education levels, or homeschooling curricula.[10]

Online Learning

Online or virtual learning frees students to learn at their own pace using the Internet, either instead of or blended with traditional bricks-and-mortar classroom learning. There are an estimated 1.8 million online course enrollments, not counting the 310,000 students nationwide enrolled in full-time online courses.[11] Research indicates that effective online learning programs keep students engaged, help improve student learning, and are cost-effective for schools.[12] Most important, online learning options can be readily tailored to the needs of individual students, allowing them more time to acquire necessary knowledge and skills if needed, without holding them back if they don't.

Private Schools

Currently, more than 5 million students are attending nearly 31,000 private schools nationwide, most of which (nearly 70 percent) have a religious affiliation.[13] A variety of parental choice programs, including voucher and tax-credit scholarships along with educational savings accounts (ESAs), are helping more than 300,000 students across the country attend the private schools of their parents' choice.[14] Close to 850,000 families in seven states are also benefiting from education tax credits and deductions that help them pay for the education they think is best for their children.[15]

PRIVATE SCHOOL PARENTAL CHOICE PROGRAMS

Parental choice programs are proliferating and have strong bi-partisan support.[16] In fact, since 2001, the year the federal No Child Left Behind Act (NCLB) was enacted, the number of students enrolled in parental choice programs has grown five-fold, from 50,000 to more than 300,000 today.[17] Rigorous research also proves parental choice works; parental choice saves money; parental choice is Constitutional; and, best of all, parental choice programs change children's lives for the better.[18] Currently 40 voucher and tax-credit scholarship programs have been enacted in 22 states, in addition to one ESA program operating in Arizona as of this writing.[19] These programs are described in greater detail in the sections that follow.

Voucher Scholarships

Elementary and secondary school voucher programs, like Pell Grants or the G.I. Bill for college students, use public dollars to fund scholarships that parents can use to send their children to schools, public or private, that they think are best. Typically, the voucher scholarship amounts are less than the per-student funding public school districts receive. There are 23 voucher scholarship programs in 14 states, including the District of Columbia. Ten voucher programs in six states are limited to low-income students: the District of Columbia, Indiana, Louisiana, North Carolina, Ohio (three programs), and Wisconsin (three programs). Of those low-income voucher programs, three also make children in failing schools a priority for scholarships: District of Columbia, Louisiana, and Ohio. Another 10 voucher programs in eight states serve students with disabilities: Florida, Georgia, Louisiana, Mississippi (two programs), North Carolina, Ohio (two programs), Oklahoma, and Utah.

The remaining three voucher programs are limited to students living in certain geographical areas. Colorado has a pilot voucher program for public school students in Douglas County. Meanwhile Vermont and Maine have the country's oldest voucher programs established in 1869 and 1873, respectively. Those programs were established so students in towns without public schools offering particular grade levels could attend private schools in nearby neighborhoods. In spite of the 2002 U.S. Supreme Court decision upholding the constitutionality of vouchers, including those for students attending religiously-affiliated private schools, the Maine and Vermont programs stand out because they expressly prohibit religious private schools from participating.[20]

Scientific research confirms that low-income students, who disproportionately attend failing public schools, using vouchers to attend private schools have higher math and reading achievement within a few years of receiving the voucher. These students also have higher high school graduation and college enrollment rates compared to their peers who didn't use vouchers. Voucher parents are also more satisfied with their children's chosen private schools, especially parents of special needs students, who report their children did better academically and socially once they transferred to their new schools.[21]

Tax-Credit Scholarships

Though similar in effect to voucher programs, tax-credit scholarship programs differ in an important way: They are funded with private dollars.[22] Under tax-credit scholarships programs, state taxpayers, both individuals and businesses, make charitable donations to non-profit scholarship-granting organizations. In turn, taxpayers receive a full or partial credit against their state income taxes for their donations.

In 2011, the Supreme Court ruled that taxpayer donations are not government funds. Responding to opponents' claim to the contrary, Justice Anthony M. Kennedy stated that the idea "that income should be treated as if it were government property even if it has not come into the tax collector's hands…. finds no basis in standing jurisprudence."[23] Thus American parents are free to use both publicly-funded voucher and privately-funded tax-credit scholarships to send their children to private schools—including religious schools—without violating the First Amendment, according to the highest court in the land.

Currently, there are 17 tax-credit scholarship programs in 13 states: Alabama, Arizona (four programs), Florida, Georgia, Iowa, Indiana, Louisiana, New Hampshire, Oklahoma, Pennsylvania (two programs), Rhode Island, South Carolina, and Virginia. As with voucher scholarship programs, all tax-credit scholarship programs except Georgia's target particular groups of students, including low-income and special-needs students, as well as those attending failing public schools.[24]

In addition to research finding that students do better in their chosen private schools, there is a significant body of research that finds tax-credit scholarship programs save taxpayers money. As with any tax-deductible program, there is an upfront revenue loss from the government's perspective. However, because private schools cost about $5,400 less per student on average than public school per-student funding, tax-credit scholarship programs become revenue-positive once a certain number of public school students transfer to private schools. Combined, the estimated annual state and local savings from operational voucher and tax-credit scholarship programs approaches $2 billion. Importantly, no credible analysis has ever concluded that these parental choice programs have a negative financial impact on the jurisdictions where they are implemented.[25]

Educational Savings Accounts (ESAs)

Arizona became the first state to enact an ESA program in 2011, called the Empowerment Scholarship Program. This program stands out for being perhaps the most straightforward and simplest parental choice program in existence. Arizona parents who do not prefer to send their children to public schools simply inform the state education agency and sign a form promising not to enroll their children during the current school year. The state then deposits an amount worth 90 percent of the amount that the state provides charter schools per-pupil, which is currently $5,300 for regular education students, into an ESA. Additional funding is provided for special needs students based on the amounts that would have been provided to their public schools for their education. Parents are then free to use those funds for their children's education, including private school tuition, online courses, private tutoring, and standardized testing fees. Any unused funds can be reserved for future educational expenses, such as college.[26]

To be eligible for the program, students must have special needs, attend or be assigned to a failing public school, have a parent who is an Active Duty member of the military, or be an adopted youth from the state's foster care system. In all, some 224,000 students are now eligible for the program, thanks to expanded eligibility requirements that took effect in the 2013-14 school year.[27]

Opponents challenged the program, claiming it was an unconstitutional transfer of public funds to private schools. In March 2014, however, the Arizona Supreme Court refused to hear their appeal of the program.[28] Arizona lawmakers further expanded the program in 2014 by making special-needs preschool children and children from military families whose parents were killed on active duty eligible to participate. Lawmakers in several other states are also considering enacting ESAs, including Iowa and Missouri.[29]

Programs such as these are empowering parents over their children's K-12 education, without the inflexibility, uniformity, and expense of federal education programs.[30] Expanding the power of parents— not government—is the proven policy path for improving student performance and parental satisfaction.

NEXT STEPS FOR POLICYMAKERS FOR IMPROVING K-12 EDUCATION

As shown above, there are a variety of ways for states and localities to give students more learning options while acting as good stewards of taxpayer dollars. What these reforms have in common is that they make schools and other educational providers accountable to parents by giving parents and education consumers greater control over the resources being spent on their children and more educational options from which to choose.

Moving forward, policymakers should be focused on expanding this trend. Arizona's ESA program provides the most promising model, by giving parents the maximum freedom to find the best educational services for their child's specific needs.

Federal policymakers should focus on advancing that goal and rolling back the onerous regulations that make it more difficult for states and localities to offer these new options.

CLEARING A PATH TO COLLEGE BY GETTING GOVERNMENT OUT OF THE WAY

Paying for college is a significant burden on Americans today. College students and their families need effective, affordable higher education options, but available evidence indicates that postsecondary productivity is poor and subsidizing student loans may be making the problem worse.

The average college senior's debt burden now approaches $30,000.[31] In fact, overall college student loan debt in the United States now surpasses $1 trillion. That's more than Americans owe on their credit cards and car loans, and that amount is projected to grow $100 billion annually.[32]

Meanwhile, unemployment rates among recent college graduates approach 9 percent, depending on students' degrees, making it difficult for them to repay loans.[33] However, the more telling figure is the 33 percent underemployment rate of recent college graduates, those ages 22 to 27 with bachelor's degrees who are working jobs that do not require degrees. According to the Federal Reserve Bank of New York, this underemployment rate has remained steady for the past 20 years throughout various ups and downs in economic and business cycles, suggesting "that about one in three college-educated workers typically holds a job that does not require a degree...[and] that it is not unusual for a significant share of college graduates to work in jobs that do not require a degree."[34] Given the current economy, it is not surprising that student loan default rates have surged to record highs, with one in seven college students in default.[35]

This wasn't supposed to happen.

For decades the federal government has been subsidizing, indirectly and now directly, college loans for students. In just the past few years alone, the federal government has also intervened to freeze college student loan interest rates. Yet recent laws to make college affordable ignore the problem of rising college costs and inefficiency. In fact, because current federal policies allow colleges to capture these additional subsidies (rather than pass them on to students), these government efforts actually make the problem worse.[36]

College tuition prices alone have been increasing about twice the general inflation rate going back to 1958. Examples of administrative and other forms of higher education bloat are plentiful. Consider the upscale dormitories, gyms, and recreational centers, not to mention the proliferating number of special interest group centers on campus, athletic teams, and lavish entertaining by public university presidents.[37] Richard Vedder, Ohio University distinguished economics professor emeritus and director of the Center for College Affordability and Productivity, aptly summed up the current state of college affairs in a recent *Wall Street Journal* interview when he said that universities:

> ...are in the housing business, the entertainment business; they're in the lodging business; they're in the food business. ... Every college today practically has a secretary of state, a vice provost for international studies, a zillion public relations specialists...My university has a sustainability coordinator whose main message, as far as I can tell, is to go out and tell people to buy food grown locally...Why?[38]

Vedder's remarks underscore yet another cost driver: burgeoning administration. One analysis finds that higher education administration is growing twice as fast as instructional staff.[39] This is significant since dozens of mid-level and senior-level administrative positions command six-figure salaries, compared to the relative handful of faculty positions that do so.[40]

Meanwhile, six-year college completion rates at public four-year institutions have remained just below 55 percent for a decade. The four-year rate has been stuck around 30 percent. That means that millions of students are spending and borrowing tens of thousands of dollars pursuing degrees, but often wind up with little more than years' worth of bills.[41]

Increased federal subsidies did little—if anything—to make college affordable since those subsidies barely keep up with steadily rising costs. Higher education officials often blame increased prices for students on reduced state funding. The American Council on Education (ACE), for example, recently argued that state budget cuts are responsible for tuition inflation. Since 1990, however, colleges used tuition increases just twice to make up for lower state subsidies, according to the Cato Institute's Neal McCluskey. In all other years tuition increases far exceeded any state funding losses.[42]

Other experts concur, noting that colleges gobble up any increases in federal student aid from the federal government because they don't contain their costs. In fact, Robert E. Martin and Andrew Gillen of the Center for College Affordability and Productivity estimate that if colleges actually did use financial aid to lower costs for students, a typical four-year college degree would cost families about $3,500 less annually, and overall higher education spending would be $59 billion less each year.[43]

BETTER INCENTIVES WOULD IMPROVE COLLEGE AFFORDABILITY

The median cost of a degree at a four-year institution is just over $68,000, and $57,200 at two-year institutions. Given high college graduate unemployment rates, parents are tapped out, and a majority of Americans (57 percent) now think colleges are not a good value for the money.[44]

Some research appears to back them up. Richard Arum and Josipa Roksa, authors of *Academically Adrift: Limited Learning on College Campuses*, found that after four years of college more than one third of undergraduates (36 percent) showed negligible improvement in critical thinking skills. Arum and Roksa note that their findings square with student accounts of their college experiences, namely:

> ...they spend increasing numbers of hours on nonacademic activities, including working, rather than on studying. They enroll in courses that do not require substantial reading or writing assignments; they interact with their professors outside of classrooms rarely, if ever; and they define and understand their college experiences as being focused more on social than on academic development.[45]

To combat high costs, Texas Governor Rick Perry challenged universities statewide during his 2011 State of the State address to design bachelor's degree programs that cost no more than $10,000, including textbooks. He suggested maximizing online instruction, innovative teaching, and rigorous efficiency improvements.[46] Two years later Gov. Perry announced that 13 universities had implemented or planned to implement a $10,000 degree program.[47] Yet, none had actually achieved the goal to date.

Rather than reduce their own costs, some universities required students to earn up to 87 of the 120 credit hours needed for their degrees at other less expensive institutions first. Other universities required students to qualify for scholarships or financial aid that would cover all the costs above $10,000, and only one of the 13 universities covered the cost of textbooks. What's more, students had limited $10,000 degree options. Noble intentions notwithstanding, the $10,000 sticker-price degree did not lower the actual cost of a four-year degree in Texas. On the contrary, as of 2013, the average cost for a bachelor's degree in Texas, including tuition, fees, books, and other supplies, was still estimated to exceed $35,000.[48]

In spite of those disappointing results, several other states have adopted or are considering similar tuition freeze plans. Florida launched a $10,000 degree program in 2012. Yet it has generated little interest among students because the degree options are limited, and not included in the advertised tuition price are several other expenses, such as textbooks, food, and housing, which combined amount to an additional $10,000 annually.[49] Several other states are also considering their own tuition freeze plans, including Iowa, Missouri, New Hampshire, New Mexico, Rhode Island, and Wisconsin.[50]

Like any price control, tuition freezes rarely contain—much less lower— costs. At best, tuition freezes are like shell games that simply reshuffle costs, not reduce them. Rather than weather the politically sensitive challenges of laying off administrative staff and increasing the course loads and class sizes of teaching staff, it's easier for colleges to simply shift or increase prices elsewhere, such as student fees. Not only are tuition freezes ineffective at lowering costs, college officials often use them to justify higher public subsidies, which help perpetuate the bloat in status-quo operations that make college so expensive in the first place.[51]

There is no reason for college to be such a burden. Better policies can encourage the creation of affordable options that give students the skills they need. Rather than tinkering around with selective loan interest rates or tuition freezes, the policy focus should be on changing the incentives so that colleges work to keep their costs down.

- **Greater Transparency from Colleges:** Requiring taxpayer-subsidized institutions to provide accurate, actionable information, including details about how their graduates fare in the job market, would help students and their families make better-informed decisions about the value of college and encourage colleges to act more economically. All postsecondary institutions participating in federal financial aid programs are now required under the

Higher Education Opportunity Act of 2008 to post a net price calculator on their websites to help students and their families determine how much they will have to pay to earn a degree based on their unique circumstances. This should be augmented so that families also have information about what outcomes they can expect for their investment, including post-degree employment rates and average earnings.

Rather than fund colleges based on how many students they enroll, state and federal policymakers should explore funding them based on how many students actually complete their degrees. To ensure colleges don't respond by simply inflating grades or reducing the rigor of their degree programs to increase the sheer volume of graduates, federal and state funding should also be linked to the number of college graduates hired by employers in their fields within a year of graduation. Colleges should also receive funding based on how much institutional aid they award to truly financially needy students.[52]

- **Differentiate College Pricing.** Not all degree programs cost the same. The costs of women's studies or philosophy degrees, for example, should be far less than engineering or pre-med degrees, which require expansive labs and equipment. It also costs more to attract professors from high-paying, high-demand private-sector fields such as engineering and medicine than it does humanities professors who do not have the same market-sector demand. A leading reason why students are charged the same tuition regardless of their degree programs is that higher education intuitions undertake a number of activities—largely subsidized by undergraduate tuition, including less popular bachelor's degree programs, graduate degree programs, research, athletics, meal programs, and housing.[53] In the private sector, a single company may have several divisions, but each one is expected to pull its own weight and turn a profit or be eliminated. Successful colleges and universities follow that principle and don't try to be all things to all people. Instead, they devote resources to supporting academic programs where they excel to help keep them affordable.[54]

Students should also not be forced to pay for other people's degree programs. Colleges should publicize the actual cost of each distinct degree program.[55] Further, students who prefer no-frills instruction from teaching assistants or online instructors should pay less tuition; while students who prefer direct instruction with the big-name tenured professors advertised in their college catalogues should pay more since the associated salary and overhead costs are higher. Additionally, colleges should also offer competency-based assessments for each course offered so students can earn credits without being stuck paying for and attending classes that cover material they've already mastered.

Finally, students should not be forced to subsidize athletic, meal, or housing programs, especially since there is no good reason these activities cannot be self-sustaining—even profitable. Colleges should publish the actual per-student cost of these programs, and students should be free to decide what—if any—they want to pay for directly through fees, not indirectly through tuition.

- **Require Alternatives to Traditional Degree Programs:** Policymakers should also demand competency-based degree programs from the institutions that participate in federal financial aid or receive state funding. Unlike traditional degree programs based on credit hours and seat time, competency-based programs allow students to progress at their own pace, taking as much time as they need to demonstrate specific knowledge- and skills-based proficiency. Currently, federal financial aid is tied to credit hours, which stifles innovation and options for students—particularly students who are working and attending school to acquire additional skills to improve their income potential.

Allowing innovative alternative higher-education providers—including online course providers—to operate introduces powerful pressure on all institutions to be efficient. Competing for students and their education dollars shifts responsibility where it belongs: on institutions themselves to eliminate waste and improve program efficiency.

- **Allow New Forms of School Financing:** Business should also be encouraged to finance their future employees directly. Sometimes referred to as human capital contracts, this financing structure allows investors to finance college students' education in exchange for a portion of their incomes after graduation. Students would sign performance contracts with the future employers who would pay for their college degree in exchange for a specified number of years of work after graduation.

IT'S TIME TO PUT PEOPLE—NOT GOVERNMENT—BACK IN CHARGE OF EDUCATION

Parents and young people don't need government meddling in their educational choices. If we want a brighter future for students of all ages, as well as the country at large, we should be investing limited public resources in people directly—not through costly, ineffective bureaucracies, which are immune to rewards for improvements and consequences for failure. At a time when Americans expect innovation, flexibility, and results in virtually every other aspect of our lives, we should also be focused on reforming the education system to encourage that kind of dynamism to provide superior educational opportunities at a lower cost to students of all ages.

CHAPTER SIX

EXPANDING CHILDCARE AND PRESCHOOL CHOICES

BY VICKI E. ALGER

Americans want all families with young children to have access to early learning opportunities that make sense for their unique circumstances. However there is little evidence that the best way to make this a reality is by expanding government's role in the provision of early education. Rather, we would be better off reducing government's involvement in early education and returning resources to parents so that they could choose the options that work best for their children, and innovative education providers would have an incentive to compete to offer high-quality services.

Unfortunately, President Obama has made expanding government's role in funding and providing preschool a pillar of his policy agenda. His $100 billion Preschool for All initiative took center stage of his 2013 State of the Union address. Democratic House Leader Nancy Pelosi also made universal preschool a top priority in her Economic Agenda for Women and Families released last summer.[1]

For all the publicity, the pricey plans went nowhere in Congress. Scaled-back funding did make its way into the omnibus spending bill passed in January 2014, including some $250 million for states to expand preschool through the Race to the Top Early Learning Challenge, along with an additional $600 million for the country's longest-running preschool program, Head Start.[2]

Now Obama says those amounts are simply a "down payment." He has proposed spending $75 billion over the next decade so all four-year-olds can attend government preschool programs. Obama also wants to spend an additional $750 million over the next year on grants for states and localities to expand their preschool programs.[3]

The rationale behind this latest preschool push, however, is deeply flawed. Last summer, Pelosi insisted that America has an early child care and education "crisis" that threatens our economy.[4] For the past two years Obama has also been adamant that expanding government preschool is critical to expanding the middle class and the economy.[5]

A majority of American mothers with preschool age children are in the labor force, and most of these working moms hold full-time jobs. Yet there is little evidence that expanding the federal government's role in providing early child care and education would improve the quality of care, student learning, or affordability—much less the economy.

On the contrary, expanding government's role in this arena is more likely to impose expensive administrative burdens, crowd out innovative, personalized non-government early childcare providers, and replace a variety of early education options with a one-size-fits-all system.

According to the government's own official evaluations of its longest-running early education program, Head Start, any learning gains quickly dissipate. Given government's poor track record in both K-12 and preprimary schooling, government's involvement should be scaled back, not expanded. And as for the economy, it's worth noting that in spite of near universal child care, most European countries have anemic economic performance compared to the United States.

Most fundamentally, the federal government has no constitutional authority over the care and education of children. That responsibility belongs to parents, who know and love their preschoolers best.

A SOLUTION IN SEARCH OF A CRISIS

Today, 60 percent of mothers with children under six years old are employed, and around 71 percent of those mothers work full-time (35 or more hours per week). On average, preschoolers with employed mothers spend 36 hours per week in child care.[6]

Expanding government preschool ignores the early care and education preferences of parents today. Available statistics suggest that the majority of preschoolers receive care from a variety of formal and informal providers and are already enrolled in a number of preprimary school programs.

Currently, nearly two-thirds of American preschoolers ages three and four are in some kind of regular childcare arrangement. Additionally, nearly two-thirds of three-, four-, and five-year-olds are already enrolled in preprimary school programs, including public and private nursery schools and kindergartens. The majority of those children (59 percent) are enrolled in full-day programs.[7]

Statistics are slightly higher for employed mothers with preschool age children. Fully 68 percent of preschoolers with employed mothers are enrolled in preprimary school programs, and most (64 percent) are enrolled in full-day programs.[8]

What should prevail, however, are the preschool preferences of parents—not politicians. Parents and relatives provide child care to almost half of the more than 20 million preschoolers nationwide—a pattern that has been consistent for more than two decades.[9] But is this situation a "crisis," or a choice?

Research indicates that a variety of priorities guide the childcare choices of parents whether they are high-earning, employed mothers or lower-income parents receiving childcare subsidies. Parents from all walks of life choose child care based on their desire for nurturing providers, safe environments, convenient locations, and educational activities.

Those priorities may help explain why employed mothers actively choose their spouses or relatives to watch their young children. They can be confident their children are loved, safe, well cared for, and happy while they're away at work. Many employed mothers may also be concerned about recent research findings that children who spend extended periods in center-based day care are more likely to display aggression and other problem behaviors.[10]

GOVERNMENT CROWDS OUT PRIVATE OPTIONS

Increasing the government's role in child care would likely impose onerous regulations on relatives who provide care, including licensing, credentialing, and home inspection mandates. Government-run child care would also tend to crowd out non family-based care, which is an important concern for parents who want to find providers that most closely reflect their beliefs about socialization, moral development, and preferred care philosophies.[11]

Currently, parents pay 57 percent of early childcare costs. Government funding accounts for another 39 percent, but that funding largely comes in the form of vouchers and tax credits—meaning funding follows children to the childcare providers parents think are best. Private sector funding accounts for the remaining 4 percent of early childcare revenue.[12] Rather than growing the government sector, we should be encouraging family saving and workplace care options, including on-site care, benefits packages, and flex schedules.

Encouraging non-government early education and child care is hardly a new—much less, partisan—idea. Nearly twenty years ago the late Stanley Greenspan, MD, professor of pediatrics and psychiatry at George Washington University, said as much at Bill Clinton's White House Conference on Early Childhood. He later reiterated his remarks in *The Washington Post*:

> Current patterns of out-of-home child care have significant limitations that endanger future generations' growing minds. A new set of guiding assumptions is necessary. We need to re-evaluate the professed value we place on children. Children and the care of them must be elevated to a higher priority, both within families and

society. This will be unrealistic for parents who, no matter how much they want to stay home, have no choice but to work. So we need to gradually bring about social arrangements which maximize at-home care of young infants by their parents.[13]

Indeed it's important to remember that millions of families—including families with modest incomes—make sacrifices to keep a family member at home because they believe that's what's best for their child. Government programs that push parents toward using institutional care devalue the contributions of these parents and make it harder for these families to make that choice.

GOVERNMENT FLUNKS THE PRESCHOOL TEST

To get an idea of the quality of care preschoolers would likely receive at the hands of government, we should review the government's track record with preschool. The federal Head Start Program, managed by the U.S. Department of Health and Human Services, was originally launched in 1965 as a six-week summer catch-up program for disadvantaged students about to enter kindergarten at a cost of $96.4 million. Today this program has 957,000 enrollees at an annual cost of nearly $8 billion.[14]

According to the two latest Head Start evaluations by HHS published in 2010 and 2012, any positive impacts associated with Head Start participation faded out as early as the end of first grade, and others dissipated by the end of third grade.[15] If government preschool can't even produce effects that last past third grade, then how is it supposed to grow the middle class and supercharge the economy?

Other longstanding preschool programs touted as models for universal, government-run preschool produced scientifically suspect benefits at best, and at huge expense. Experts involved with those programs also caution that they were never intended for students from middle class families and likely would have no positive academic impacts.[16]

Consider the often-cited High/Scope Perry Preschool Project, conducted from 1962 through 1965. Back then project researchers asserted that taxpayers would get a $7.16 return for every dollar spent—except neither they nor the toddlers got the promised bang for the buck. Aside from the weak scientific methods used, the results have never been replicated—even though the program cost around $19,000 per toddler in today's dollars.[17] Moreover, the project focused on just 58 disadvantaged preschoolers with mental retardation, and experts caution that this is a poor model to universalize. In fact, David Weikart, past president of the High/Scope Educational Research Foundation, told *U.S. News & World Report*, "For middle-class youngsters with a good economic basis, most programs are not able to show much in the way of difference."[18]

The Carolina Abecedarian Project, another often-cited study, began in 1972 and involved 57 infants averaging about four months old. These children received intensive home interventions that lasted until they entered kindergarten. As with the Perry Preschool Project, results were never replicated, and experts noted that after nearly five years there was very little difference between participants and non-participants.[19]

A federally funded longitudinal study of the Chicago Child-Parent Center Program began in the mid-1980s and at least had a larger study group—more than 1,000 low-income children. But those children participated with their parents in extensive workshops and tutoring—again far more than just preschool.[20] Like the Perry Preschool and Abecedarian Projects, the Chicago program analysis used suspect methodologies. That didn't stop other research organizations from insisting that every dollar invested would yield returns ranging from $2.62 to $11.[21] It also didn't curb enthusiastic claims that preschool boosts high-school graduation rates, and slashes arrest rates.[22]

For all the attention lavished on these programs, they are not at all suitable national models—and government-preschool proponents know it. Just weeks before the President unveiled his latest preschool-for-all plan, the *New York Times'* Nicholas Kristof tried to put a fresh spin on the Head Start fade-out dilemma, saying that "early education has always had an impact not through cognitive gains but through long-term improvements in life outcomes."[23] He cited two studies purportedly claiming positive, long-term life outcomes for preschool students, but he neglected to mention that the researchers could only *estimate* the *likelihood* of better outcomes on participants because only short-term evaluations are conducted—even though Head Start began in 1965.[24]

None of this has stopped Obama, Pelosi, Kristof, and others from linking any number of long-term benefits to government preschool, from more than 10 to 1 rates of return on taxpayer subsidized "investment," to reduced incarceration rates, and higher college attendance rates.

In the real world, private investors demand proofs of concept before they invest their hard-earned dollars. Government programs should be held to the same standard regarding any program it seeks to implement or expand—especially when those programs affect children.

EMPOWER PARENTS RATHER THAN GROWING GOVERNMENT

Childcare for four-year-olds ranges from $3,700 to more than $12,000 annually, depending on where parents live and whether they prefer home- or center-based care.[25] On average, families with children under five pay $179 per week (over $9,300 a year) for child care. Yet less than 11 percent of preschool parents receive help to pay for child care from any source, including 7 percent who receive help from the government. Rather than encourage reliance on federal subsidies, two existing programs could be readily expanded.[26]

The Child Care Tax Credit allows employed parents to claim up to $3,000 per child and up to $6,000 for two or more children annually in eligible childcare expenses so they can work.[27] Alternatively, parents can take advantage of flexible spending accounts (FSAs) offered by their employers. An FSA lets parents set aside up to $5,000 that is deducted from their gross annual salaries. Funds are free from federal income tax, as well as Social Security and Medicare taxes. However, the $5,000 cap is not doubled for married couples filing jointly, and any unused funds go back to employers.[28]

Policymakers could seek to reduce the burden of paying for childcare, for example, by allowing all parents to deduct 100 percent of their eligible childcare expenses against their federal income taxes. FSA options could also be expanded by removing the marriage penalty, lifting annual caps, and allowing rollovers for unused funds. Employer matches could be encouraged by allowing businesses to claim credits against their taxes for their contributions to employees' FSAs. Similar credits could be given to businesses that offer on-site care, offer flex schedules and telecommuting to employees, or offer childcare benefits packages.

It should be noted, however, that all these tax programs advantage working parents over those who make a sacrifice to keep a parent at home to care for their children. To help all parents better care for their children, policymakers could look to reduce the overall tax burden on families, by increasing deductions for dependents and by lowering tax rates across the board.

Lawmakers can also facilitate a more diverse, dynamic early education sector by giving parents direct control over the resources already spent on early education that currently go through the state.

On average state, local, and federal funding per public preschool student amounts to $4,600, while Head Start funding for three- and four-year-olds averages nearly $7,800.[29] Proponents insist that the federal government should match state preschool expenditures up to $10,000, for an estimated annual cost of $98.4 billion over the next decade, plus an additional $12.3 billion annually once the match program is fully implemented.[30]

Rather than expanding the unsuccessful Head Start program, parents should be empowered to choose the preschool options they think are best.

Lawmakers could adopt Early Education Savings Accounts (EESAs) modeled after Arizona's successful K-12 ESA program. Instead of funneling more money into Head Start, lawmakers would deposit what would have been spent on a child into parents' EESAs, adjusted according to family income and size.[31] States should also consider enacting Early Education Tax Credit scholarship programs, which would allow individual and corporate taxpayers to claim a dollar-for-dollar credit against their taxes for donations to non-profit scholarship-granting organizations.[32]

Most importantly, lawmakers should recognize that with a real unemployment rate hovering between 11 and 13 percent and a national debt approaching $18 trillion, spending billions of dollars more to further expand the government into early child care and education makes no sense.[33] Women want the benefits of a diverse economy, and employed mothers want their children to benefit from diverse early care and learning opportunities—not more wasteful, ineffective government programs.

LET'S HEED SOME LESSONS FROM K-12 SCHOOLING

Before pushing for more government spending on and oversight of preschool and childcare programs, lawmakers should consider the experience of K-12 public education, as was described in the preceding chapter.

Public schools now spend an average of nearly $13,700 annually per pupil.[34] Yet in spite of increased spending and government oversight of how schools operate, student performance has remained flat for decades.[35] Increasingly Americans across the country have come to realize that the solution to improving education is expanding options for parents, not expanding government.

That's why today more than 300,000 schoolchildren nationwide are benefiting from innovative parental choice programs, including publicly-funded voucher scholarship, privately-funded tax-credit scholarship, and educational savings account (ESA) programs.[36] Together with homeschooling, virtual schools, and public charter schools, these private school choice programs are successfully restoring personalized learning options for students. Specifically, parental choice programs help raise academic performance and high school graduation rates.[37] A greater variety of schools means parents have a better chance at finding schools that more closely reflect their beliefs and work better for their children.

American children deserve a first-rate education. Sadly, the federal government rarely advances that goal. The federal Head Start program has actually proven to be a dead start that at best leaves children no better off than when they started, but has cost children and taxpayers dearly. Consider that since 1965 the number of enrollees has not quite doubled, from 561,000 to 957,000 today, but the cost has increased more than six-fold in real terms from $1,280 per enrollee in 1965 to more than $8,000 now.

The last thing our country can afford is spending more on programs that at best aren't needed, and at worst, don't work. Most parents prefer family, at-home or small childcare and learning centers rather than institutional daycare centers, which are typically the vehicles for most government programs. Expanding government's role in providing preschool and child care may mean fewer choices for parents.

There are better ways to encourage more affordable, innovative childcare and preschool options, beginning with empowering parents over the education of their children at every age.

CHAPTER SEVEN

FREEDOM AND A FULL MENU OF CHOICE

BY JULIE GUNLOCK

We live in safe, healthy and abundant times. Americans have never had such easy access to food, medicine, and the basic necessities of life. Our air and water is cleaner than ever before, most infectious diseases have been eradicated because of vaccines, and poverty rates continue to decline. The crime rate is back to the level it was in the 1960s and literacy rates continue to rise. Children born today will live longer than their parents, and most of those years will be spent disease-free.

Despite this good news, most American women believe the world is becoming a far more dangerous, less healthy place, and some believe the government should intervene to make the world safer.[1] Much of the anxiety women feel is fueled by the constant drum beat of warnings that come from environmental and public health organizations who tell women that the food they eat, the household and personal care products they use, and the habits they practice threaten their health and the health of their children. These groups understand that if you get the public nervous enough, they're more likely to acquiesce to government regulations.

This tactic is used to advance big government generally, but in this chapter I'll consider three recent policy initiatives advanced by alarmism: Regulations on the food industry, government anti-obesity measures, and reforms to the Federal School Lunch Program. The American public was fed a steady diet of exaggerations about how failing to pass these three measures would result in terrible consequences and would lead to a far less fiscally sound, less healthy American public.

Of course, these are only three examples—only a small sampling of the near constant warnings of danger coming from those who seek more control over how Americans choose to live their lives. Women in particular are targeted for warnings about food and common products like shampoo, deodorant, plastic food containers, household cleaners, and products used by their children like toys, playground equipment, Halloween costumes, baby bottles and sippy-cups, crib mattresses and bed sheets and even baby soap and lotion. Even things as benign as garden hoses have been cast as silent killers by environmental activists eager to see more onerous regulations on the chemical industry. The message being sent to women is simple: You're not safe, and only the state can protect you.

For instance, the American Academy of Pediatrics 2010 list of "high risk" foods includes apples, chewing gum, peanut butter, marshmallows, nuts, popcorn, raw carrots, sausages, seeds, grapes and hot dogs. The AAP wants the government to require food manufacturers to place warning labels on food packages in order to reduce injuries due to choking. Yet, is it really possible to make every food child proof? Shouldn't we instead advise parents to cut food into child-safe sizes? Perhaps parents should be reminded that a good way to prevent choking is to explain to a child the importance of eating slowly and thoroughly chewing. But according to the AAP, it's government that should be doing more, more, more to protect kids. One AAP spokesman reasoned that since parents can't watch children every second, the best way to protect kids is to design these risks out of existence. But is that really realistic? Can we ever really design a world free of risk?

Of course not.

Therefore, the best way to protect our children is to teach them how to face and mitigate these risks. Children who are aware that life comes with risks will be far better prepared to face them and make good decisions.

Yet alarmists often confuse small potential risk with true, realistic threats. If we take the logic of the alarmists, we should avoid anything that could potentially cause any injury or discomfort. For instance, zoos contain dangerous animals like lions and tigers and bears (Oh my!). These animals are indeed a hazard and if these dangerous animals were allowed to roam free among the people, it would indeed be hazardous to visit the zoo. But, because zoo animals are placed in an enclosure or cage, while it remains a potential hazard, humans aren't truly at risk because the risks have been mitigated.

Alarmists exaggerate potential risks and focus on outcomes that have little relevance to the real world. Water consumed through a garden hose may contain trace chemicals that pose a threat only if consumed in large quantities. But this tells us nothing about the danger (or lack thereof) of taking a drink from the hose on a summer afternoon while playing in the sprinkler. The risk associated with drinking water all day everyday solely through a garden hose—a situation that would never occur in the real world—is misleadingly repackaged to the public as the risk they face anytime they turn on the hose.

There is tremendous harm caused by this alarmism. These "it's good for you" government efforts have the deleterious affect of infantilizing Americans to the point that they fail to recognize their own good instincts and stop trusting themselves to make common sense decisions. It distracts people from the real risks they face, often leads to worse health outcomes, creates great expense for consumers, and makes our lives less free and fun.

The best way to ensure the world continues to improve is by allowing the market to respond to individual preferences. Regulations should focus on eliminating true, substantiated hazards and requiring businesses to inform consumers about real risks, but otherwise American businesses and consumers should be given the freedom to innovate, produce and buy more products that will improve our lives and advance our standard of living.

FREE MARKETS IMPROVE LIVES

To understand how choice and competition is improving the lives of Americans by offering higher quality and more diversity, one need only take a stroll down the chip and snack aisle at your local grocery store.

Just glancing at the shelves, it's easy to see how nearly every conceivable diet need, taste preference, and environmental conviction is covered. From full-fat to non-fat, baked and fried, to reduced- and no-salt, organic, multigrain, non-GMO, gluten-free, vegetarian, vegan, nut-free, nut-filled, trans fat-free, flavored, vitamin-fortified, protein-packed, and sustainably-produced and packaged—most foodie proclivities are covered by food manufacturers who are eager to please the American consumer.

Yet, some critics claim the food industry must be regulated to better serve the consumer or, as Mayor Bloomberg envisions, to stop providing customers the products he and other food activists deem unhealthy. These critics have called on government officials at every level to regulate the food industry—from cigarette-style limits on certain type of marketing techniques, to bans on select ingredients, to ingredient- and product-specific taxes.

Under the Obama Administration, the Food and Drug Administration (FDA) has been eager to pursue these regulations in order to help Americans make "better" food decisions and ultimately turn them into healthier Americans. For example, in 2011, the FDA announced it planned to require food manufacturers to cut the amount of salt used in processed food in order to reduce cardiovascular disease. Agency officials were convinced that less salt consumption through government fiat would result in a lower mortality rate.

Yet, according to more recent research (which was ignored by the FDA), there is little evidence that limiting salt reduces the risk for cardiovascular diseases in people with normal or high blood pressure. Other studies warn that low sodium diets might actually harm individuals with normal blood pressure, particularly the elderly.[2] And according to a 2014 study from the University of Copenhagen Hospital in Denmark and published in the American Journal of Hypertension, the daily sodium intake guidelines offered by the US Centers for Disease Control and Prevention are "excessively and unrealistically low."[3]

The FDA backed off salt regulations (for now), but the Agency's preoccupation with protecting Americans from their own free choices continues. In 2013, the agency announced it was working on regulations that would ban a type of oil called trans fats used in many baked goods and confections.[4] FDA Commissioner Margaret A. Hamburg offered an openly paternalistic justification for the move, saying:

> The FDA's action today is an important step toward protecting more Americans from the potential dangers of trans fat. Further reduction in the amount of trans fat in the American diet could prevent an additional 20,000 heart attacks and 7,000 deaths from heart disease each year—a critical step in the protection of Americans' health.[5]

Banning trans fats from processed foods might seem like a no-brainer. Unlike olive oil and other so-called "healthy fats," trans fats (a lipid produced by pumping hydrogen into liquid vegetable oils to make it solid and stable) raises bad (LDL) cholesterol levels while lowering good (HDL) cholesterol levels. Few debate the conclusion that it's bad stuff. And this is why food manufacturers have been removing trans fats from their products for years. In fact, the pressure to remove trans fats from processed food has been so aggressive that today it's quite difficult to find food made with trans fats.

So, why does the FDA still find it necessary to trot out this new regulation on trans fats? Because it can, of course, and because trans fats do persist in a few foods no one would ever mistake for health foods. Those foods include doughnuts, movie-theater popcorn, frozen pizzas, candy, shelf-stable frostings, coffee creamers, and refrigerated dough products like biscuits and cinnamon buns.

Considering that one generally puts these foods in the "items-one-should-not-eat-too-much" category, perhaps the better role for government is to act as an educator about these types of fats and to advise consumers to limit their consumption of such foods, rather than putting these manufacturers out of business and those companies' employees out of work. And that will happen. When the trans fat ban was passed in New York City, some ethnic restaurants and small bakeries were hard hit. The owner of one New York bakery told the *New York Times* that his costs increased 20 percent when he had to eliminate trans fats from his baked goods.[6]

Although these "it's-good-for-you" regulations sometimes sound good, women—the primary food shoppers in most families—must understand that consumers are already provided a wide variety of choices in the grocery store. Finding low-salt and trans fat-free food is easy. Food manufacturers are aware that consumers want a variety of choices, including healthy options.

And in fact, processed food is getting healthier. Why? Because people are demanding healthier food. In addition to removing billions of calories from processed food products, the food industry is reporting record profits in the category of healthy snacks.[7] And, according to market research, healthier food consumption is forecast to rise by more than a fifth in 2014.[8] That's good news for consumers and an important lesson on the power of consumer demand over do-gooder government mandates.

BIG-GOVERNMENT'S APPROACH TO REDUCING OBESITY

During the debate on ObamaCare, supporters of the administration would often explain that the United States was in the midst of an obesity crisis that would bankrupt the country because of the rising medical costs associated with treating the millions of Americans with obesity-related diseases. By making obesity a collective burden, being fat was no longer your own a private affliction, it was a national budgetary concern and the legitimate purview of government officials.

Yet, while supporters were busy explaining how ObamaCare would "solve" the skyrocketing medical cost issue, they rarely addressed how nationalizing health care would affect the crisis itself: Would the obesity crisis be reversed under ObamaCare? Would people suddenly begin eating right and getting moderate exercise? Would nationalized health care create incentives to eat right? Or would it make it worse?

Sometimes when considering economic issues, it's important to take a step back and consider human nature. After all, humans are not widgets. People respond to incentives and take into account the expected outcomes from their decisions. In a truly free society, people must be free not only to make good decisions (I'll order the salad) but also bad ones (I'll order the burger and fries), so long as they also bear the consequences of those choices. That's why one way to tackle the obesity issue isn't by centralizing health care; it's to create market-based reforms that will encourage healthier behavior by giving Americans an incentive to live healthier.

Consider these two, competing systems for discouraging obesity.

Under ObamaCare, the government has an interest in controlling obesity-related costs. This means the government has a direct interest in your eating decisions, and gives policymakers an opening to try to encourage behavior it deems good and discourage choices it considers bad. Note that this system also gives government an interest in all other health-related decisions that Americans would instinctively recognize as none of government's business, from with whom one has sexual encounters, how frequently, and what kind, to how many hours one sleeps each night and how much time one spends in the sun or sitting on the couch.

Rather than giving government an interest in all manner of people's personal life-style decisions, under a more free-market health care system, which would detangle the links between the government and employer-provided health insurance companies, individuals, not the government and not employers, would be responsible for obtaining insurance and health care that makes sense for their situations, and they would bear the costs and reap the rewards of their decisions about their behaviors. This free-market system creates a natural incentive (versus a government order) to stay healthy because in doing so, an individual's health care costs are lower and he or she can spend more on other items.

This is common sense. When one is free to take risks—be it by smoking, wearing 7-inch platform heels, skydiving, or ordering steak frites with a side of fatty béarnaise sauce—people who understand they are ultimately responsible for the consequences of that decision may do it a bit less, particularly if it costs them money in the form of higher health care premiums. However, if the federal government is picking up the tab for these risky behaviors, there is less reason to seek to stay healthy. Bring on the béarnaise!

Look at this in another way: When the government makes people's risky behavior (I'm wearing insanely high heels) a matter of community burden (taxpayers are responsible for the rise in foot injuries), the government has an interest in preventing those behaviors that cause such injuries. Under this system, perhaps the government (in trying to be good stewards of taxpayer dollars) would see fit to ban certain high-heeled shoes. Perhaps the government would consider putting certain time limits on high heels being worn (they can only be worn two hours per day). Perhaps the government will require you to carry sneakers with you so that you can change into more comfortable shoes when walking to the metro. Perhaps the government could throw the whole Sex and the City cast in jail for encouraging a generation of young girls to wear arch-crushing shoes.

Seem unrealistic? Maybe. But consider what government officials are already doing to quell what they see as other risky lifestyle behaviors. In New York City, Mayor Michael Bloomberg created a number of "it's-good-for-you" policies, including smoking bans (which include city parks and public plazas), sugary beverage size restrictions (later found unconstitutional), trans fat bans, anti-salt public relations campaigns, regulations on tanning salons, calorie counts on menus, regulations on what food items can be donated to homeless shelters (no doughnuts, thank you very much!), and regulations designed to cajole women into breast feeding. The result of these nanny-state policies hasn't been to improve the health of New Yorkers. Rather, it's been to infantilize and embarrass the citizens of New York.

Inspired by Bloomberg's shenanigans, other cities have followed suit, as have lawmakers and other officials in the federal government. In fact, the ObamaCare legislation itself included a provision requiring chain restaurants with 20 or more locations to post calorie information on their menus. This measure was included ostensibly to reign in health care costs related to obesity, but there is scant evidence to suggest that this information will encourage people to make healthier choices.

According to a 2011 Duke-NUS Medical School study on the impact of menu labeling requirements, customers' choices stayed the same despite the information provided to them.[9] Another 2011 study by New York University's School of Medicine found that menu labels have little effect on the food choices made by either teens or their parents.[10] And a 2009 joint New York University and Yale University study found that only half the customers noticed the prominently posted calorie counts.[11] Yet, these regulations will certainly have at least one important impact: According to the Food Marketing Institute, this menu-labeling regulation would cost the industry $1 billion in the first year of implementation.[12] And those costs will be passed on to consumers largely in the form of higher prices.

As government becomes more involved in managing America's health care system and responsible for a growing portion of related costs, what measure can we expect from government officials desperate to bring down the budget? Will the government begin to track individuals' BMIs and fine them for costing the taxpayers more? Will gym memberships be mandated? Will we be subjected to home checks to ensure we're stocking our cupboards with only the items found on the USDA's list of dietary guideline-approved food? Will home-packed meals be banned from public schools in favor of government-approved school lunches?

Obesity certainly deserves to be studied and addressed, but increasing government intervention is unlikely to reduce obesity. According to the CDC, obesity rates overall are no longer increasing. The rates of children who are overweight and obese have remained stable at around 32 percent and 17 percent, respectively, for a decade.[13] If we want this trend to continue and obesity to decline, we must continue to detangle the government from health care costs and make free-market reforms to the health care system so that people will truly be encouraged to make good and healthy decisions.

SERVING COMPETITION FOR HEALTHIER SCHOOL LUNCHES

In 2010, First Lady Michelle Obama announced the creation of the Let's Move Campaign, the goal of which was to reverse childhood obesity within a decade. According to Mrs. Obama, improving and expanding the federal school lunch program was one way to reach this lofty goal.

This would be no easy task. The Federal School Lunch Program has a long history of mismanagement and has been plagued with charges of waste, fraud and abuse. And far from providing kids nutritious meals, the program had become a punch line, well known for providing food high in calories and low in nutritional content. Despite decades of Congressional attempts to address these issues through more government funding and oversight, the bloated program seemed impervious to any sort of meaningful reform.

Yet, this dismal record of more government micromanaging meant little to an Obama Administration which doubled-down on the liberal strategy: pump more money into the broken program with fingers crossed that things would improve.

But it didn't. In fact, the school lunch program has gotten worse since the passage of the Healthy and Hunger-Free Kids Act in 2010, which funneled billions of taxpayer dollars into the system. The bill seemed simple: make lunches healthier by increasing leafy greens and healthy carbohydrates while limiting sugar, salt and fat. The bill also set one-size-fits-all, per-meal calorie requirements, allotting 650 calories to K through fifth graders, 700 calories to sixth through eighth graders, and 850 calorie meals for high school-aged kids.

While putting kids into these separate monolithic blocks might work on a USDA dry-erase board stapled to a conference room wall, in practice, these rigid rules caused major problems for a diverse school population. For instance, these calorie requirements didn't account for a child's specific age (a Kindergartener eats a lot less than a fifth grader), sex, height, or activity level. (A 110-pound high school cheerleader doesn't require as many calories as a 280-pound high school football linebacker.)

Other problems with the school lunch reforms persisted. The most obvious: Kids simply detested the "new and improved" food being served. Some schools, so worried about dropping participation, opted out of the school lunch program all together. Other schools, worried about the considerable waste being generated (both because children were throwing away whole trays full of food and because kids simply wouldn't eat what was being served) made agreements with local food banks to donate all the unwanted food. At least someone was enjoying the First Lady's food.[14]

The truly galling part of this story is that the Obama administration had an opportunity to bring real and lasting change to the broken school lunch program. The Administration's failure to encourage innovative, free-market approaches to lunch reforms that would still appeal to children and teenagers is truly disappointing considering the goodwill the First Lady had at the time she was pushing for the passage of the bill. This was a rare time when meaningful change could have taken place.

Fortunately, communities are already working to create changes in some school districts. Tired of waiting for the federal government, some schools have integrated free-market solutions into their programs, resulting in successful reforms.

For instance, in 2010, the Seattle School District received a federal stimulus grant (ponder that for a moment) to work on improving school lunches. The school district chose to retain a private company called Tom Douglas Restaurants to design healthy and satisfying meals using a per-meal budget of $1.10 (beating the cost of federally reimbursement rate of $2.72 for free meals, $2.32 for reduced-price).[15] Today, this public-private system is working in 85 Seattle schools and serves 19,000 lunches each day. The reviews are so positive that Seattle schools are often held up as a model of reforming school lunch programs.[16]

Another way to make school lunches healthier is to separate the school lunch program from farm subsidies. Nationwide, 15 to 20 percent of the food served at schools comes from USDA commodities supplied through a program called USDA Foods, which is administered by the USDA's Food and Nutrition Service (FNS).[17] This depression-era program was designed to help stabilize the farm economy in the 1930s yet it persists and has grown to so large that in 2009 USDA Foods provided nearly $1.2 billion worth of commodity food to school districts.[18]

So what kind of food makes up these commodities? While Michelle Obama has been busy implying school lunch ladies just don't understand how to make healthy food, the blame really lies with the USDA which sends chicken nuggets, fried pork patties, French fries, canned cheese, as well as a variety of branded foods (like Tyson Mini Snackers, Pizza Stuffed Meatball Bites, and Smuckers Uncrustables sandwiches) to schools. Contrary to what Mrs. Obama says, when kids eat this food at school, it's not the result of some clueless lunch lady with a love of processed food. It's because this food is what the lunch lady was sent by the very same government telling her she's doing it all wrong.

If we want kids to eat healthier, Congress should eliminate the commodity program and replace it with direct funding to schools so that they can purchase their own food on the open market. This gives more control to local officials and eliminates the overhead costs associated with transporting commodities across the country. Analysis from Michigan State University supports this strategy:

> Over the last two decades, many school food professionals have questioned the overall value and efficiency of the commodity system. Some argue that making all of their purchases with cash would give them more freedom and choice, including the choice to purchase more foods locally. Freed from the program's significant overhead costs, they ask, might they actually have more money to spend on feeding children? One recent economic analysis of school purchasing across Minnesota in 2008-09 supports this view. It found that once full procurement costs—including processing, handling, transportation, administrative labor, warehousing, inventory investment, and cost of risk to

hold inventory—were assessed, commercial products on average were estimated to be 9% less expensive than equivalent USDA commodity products.[19]

The most radical, free-market strategy for improving school lunches will likely never find congressional support, but it is a system that could really work to improve school lunches. Full privatization of the school lunch program would accomplish three important goals: It would reduce costs for feeding children in need; It would be more efficient because private businesses could simply be fired for waste and fraud, and; Lastly, parents, teachers and local school officials would have a direct say on what types of foods kids are eating, by choosing businesses that stay within set rules.

Under this system, school cafeterias would be transformed into mini-food courts where a handful of private restaurants could provide parent- and school-approved food. Participating restaurants would have to adhere to these rules (perhaps some schools would ban fried food, others might say kids can only get fresh fruit and yogurt for dessert, others might limit sugary drinks or refined carbohydrates, some would offer salad bars, still others require whole wheat bread and pasta products). There's a natural incentive built in for these businesses to do what they're told. After all, the USDA's federal school lunch program serves over 5 million meals a day to over 32 million kids. What company wouldn't want a share of that customer base?

Of course, the best way to feed children appropriately is for parents—who know their children's needs and preferences, and have the most interest in their long-term health—to pack them a homemade meal that they take with them to school. But since the school lunch program is unlikely to go away, we should all hope for a properly managed system that provides good food to kids in need without wasting taxpayer dollars.

ALARMISM: KILLING INNOVATION AND FREEDOM

Proponents of big government have a powerful rhetorical tool they use to push their agenda: fear. This narrative worked well to convince Americans that rising health care costs due to obesity would bankrupt the country.

It pulled at the heart strings of Americans who were told the First Lady's lunch reforms were the only thing standing in between the nation's obese children and a life of pain and misery. Fear helped convince Americans that the food industry works to harm them and their families and that government action would solve the problem. Alarmists are banking on fooling the American public into believing we're living in more dangerous times. They hope, once scared, someone at some point will say the magic words: "Something must be done!"

What good-hearted Americans don't always realize is that that "something" usually takes the form of job-crushing, price-hiking, choice-limiting, fun-killing, freedom-stealing regulations.

Do Americans really want that? Do free men and women want to live under the thumb of do-gooder government officials determined to regulate and fine you into good behavior? Do Americans want their decisions questioned by Washington bureaucrats who claim to know what's best for their children?

Free people should reject this vision of the relationship between citizens and the state. Yes, freedom isn't always perfect. It means that some people will make poor decisions, including eating foods and engaging in behaviors that are bad for them. Yet trying to do away with this and cajole people into following the model prescribed by the government is a far greater danger. In doing so, we all become the children of government, a little more dependent, a little more risk averse and much more paranoid about things and activities not approved by our government minders.

That's a sure fire way to kill innovation, to make us less healthy society and...dare I say it, to make our country more dangerous.

That's the real cause for alarm.

CHAPTER EIGHT

ENERGY EMPOWERMENT

BY JILLIAN MELCHIOR

Energy policy isn't just energy policy. Dull as it may sound on first pass to the casual reader, few issues have such widespread implications for the nation as a whole. Energy has an impact on the economy, American foreign policy, and the environment. We want policies that help ensure that Americans have access to reliable, affordable energy sources, reduce dependence on foreign sources of oil—particularly on countries with interests that conflict with ours—and protect environmental resources.

The good news is, energy policy is one area where the United States is entirely and dramatically *winning* and moving toward realizing that vision.

Moreover, our energy eminence is likely to grow even more overwhelmingly strong, as long as bad policies don't get in the way. The creative shenanigans of those who stand to profit off destructive policies may make for good reading and sadly too often good politics, but they could significantly limit the potential of one of America's biggest assets.

UNDERSTANDING FRACKING

To understand America's energy issues and to craft sound energy policy, it's essential to have a good understanding of "fracking"—or "hydraulic fracturing," in stodgier, more technical language—a much-maligned process that, when paired with horizontal drilling, has singlehandedly revolutionized America's energy situation.

Enormous reserves of natural gas and oil are trapped beneath American soil in shale, a dense stone formation where oil and gas originate. By the Energy Information Administration's best estimates, the United States is home to more than 2,303 trillion cubic feet of potential natural-gas resources[1] (which, presuming a 2009 rate of consumption, is 110 years' worth of natural gas),[2] as well as 220.2 billion barrels of oil[3]—but until recently, most of that energy was inaccessible. Fracking involves the "fracturing" of energy-storing rock formations, allowing producers access to these reserves.

Though fracking has become controversial in recent years, it's actually a fairly old process—and one that makes today's tactics look benign.

In the 1860s, a veteran of the Mexican War and Civil War named Edward A. Roberts was reportedly inspired by the artillery-shell damage he'd seen in combat, and he decided to drop an "exploding torpedo" made of up to 20 pounds of gun powder down a well.[4] After it detonated, he used large amounts of water to further pry apart the stone above the shale layer, releasing trapped energy reserves in the process. The idea was a success, and soon, Roberts was selling his patented torpedoes to energy producers for up to $200 apiece, plus royalties.[5]

Though the process was soon adopted by major mining companies, safety was lacking—especially when nitroglycerin came to replace gun powder. In fact, one observer noted in 1869 that "the chap who struck it a hard rap might as well avoid trouble among his heirs by having had his will written and a cigar-box ordered to hold such fragments as his weeping relatives could pick up from the surrounding district."[6]

Happily for energy prospectors who wanted to keep their corporeal assets intact, methods gradually improved. In 1946, Stanolind—short for Standard Oil of Indiana—put together one of the first-ever research groups to improve drilling processes. They pioneered the process of fracking with water and sand, and their methods caught on across the industry; by the 1950s, scientific papers discussed more than 100,000 wells being fracked in American borders.[7]

But it wasn't until decades later that energy companies learned how to drill directly into the shale itself, rather than just the rock above, unlocking the fundamental source where oil and gas are "baked." George Mitchell of Mitchell Energy & Development is known today as the father of fracking, but his quest to access the energy reserves trapped in shale formations stretched over two decades, beginning in the 1980s.[8]

Mitchell's discovery was a classic American success story, explains Russell Gold, author of *The Boom: How Fracking Ignited the American Energy Revolution and Changed the World.* He wanted to access energy from its primary source, and he was willing to support creative experiments that might help get him there. Eventually, a young engineer petitioned Mitchell to let him water-frack a shale formation, receiving permission to work on three wells. All were complete failures. The engineer returned to Mitchell and asked for three more to experiment on. The fourth failed, as did the fifth—and "the sixth finally hits it out of the park," Gold says. "That's the turning point. That is when the modern petroleum industry realizes that it can frack the shales."[9]

Devon Energy bought Mitchell Energy & Development in 2001, then combining its shale-fracking techniques with horizontal drilling. Before, drilling could only happen vertically, allowing access to only a small section of all the rocks that held natural gas inside.[10] But by running through the shale formations horizontally, access to the energy resources was maximized.

These combined processes launched an energy revolution, and over the past decade, the United States has found itself a major energy producer, reversing a longtime trend of energy decline. One-fourth of all natural gas production in 2012 was drawn out of shale formations,[11] which brought natural gas prices to their lowest level in 10 years.[12] Meanwhile, in 2012, the United States extracted two million barrels of shale oil every day—when in 1999, it extracted none at all.[13]

The economic impact of this energy boom has been explosive.

Employment in the sector increased by a whopping 40 percent between 2008 and 2013, despite the terrible economy, and even as private-sector jobs overall grew by only 1 percent.[14] In 2012, oil and natural gas supported more than 2.1 million jobs, a number only expected to increase.[15]

Women filled around a third of the new jobs in oil and natural gas in 2013.[16] Overall, the oil and gas industry is expected to add 185,000 more female workers by 2030. Moreover, these are high-paid, high-skilled openings; between 2010 and 2030, nearly 70,000 petroleum engineer, managerial and other white-collar energy jobs will be filled by women, according to one credible report's estimate.[17]

Even for women not working in the energy sector, the boom has had a positive effect. In 2012, the rising production of unconventional oil and gas brought down the prices of both energy and commodities that use it as an input, leaving the average household with an extra $1,200 in disposable income. As development accelerates even more, by 2015, American households will see more than $2,000 freed up yearly.[18]

Furthermore, the energy boom has added prodigally to the public purse, helping pay for government services at the local, state and federal levels. In 2012 alone, the oil and gas sector paid nearly $75 billion in taxes.[19]

But America's energy boom has also been felt around the globe—a fact that works particularly to the benefit of the United States and its liberal-democracy allies.

In October 2013, the United States became a net producer of oil for the first time since 1995. That same fall, we extracted more oil than even Saudi Arabia, becoming the largest producer on earth.[20] Furthermore, in

2012, we surpassed Russia in natural-gas production, also becoming the world's top producer.[21]

One of the immediate effects has been to reduce American dependence on foreign energy. In 2013, the United States reversed a longstanding trend, exporting more oil than it had imported for the first time in nearly 20 years.[22] In fact, if current resources are fully developed, the United States could meet all of its liquid fuel needs with North American energy by 2024, according to the American Petroleum Institute.

In addition to helping reduce our dependence on foreign energy, the American boom also has the potential to reduce friendly nations' dependence on gas and oil derived from less savory nations. Right now, Europe gets about one-third of its natural gas from Russia—a fact Putin uses to bully the region. American energy exports threaten Russia's energy dominance in Europe, potentially reducing exports of Russian gas by 25 percent.[23]

American energy also has the potential to improve the environment, both at home and across the world.

In 2012, natural gas provided 30 percent of American power, up from 19 percent in 2005.[24] Even ExxonMobil has predicted that worldwide, natural gas will overtake coal, becoming the second most common fuel in use.[25] That matters because natural gas is, by a long stretch, the cleanest of all traditional energy sources; for example, when natural gas is used to generate electricity instead of coal, it cuts carbon emissions by a third.[26]

Critics note that this doesn't take into account methane emissions at well sites—but a recent study by the University of Texas at Austin—the most comprehensive ever done—found that the Environmental Protection Agency had overstated methane leaks by at least 20 percent. Meanwhile, ever-improving "completion" technology has proven capable of catching 99 percent of emissions at energy-extraction sites.[27]

As natural gas crowds out other traditional energy sources, the air gets cleaner. Between 2005 and 2012, America's energy-related carbon emissions dropped by 12 percent.[28] And 2012 also saw the lowest level of carbon emissions in two decades, which the Energy Information Administration attributed in large part to "a decline in coal-fired electricity generation, due largely to historically low natural gas prices."[29]

Despite these substantial environmental benefits, green groups have targeted fracking, claiming it is dangerous and irresponsible. Sierra Club director Michael Brune once wrote that natural gas was "a gangplank to a destabilized climate and an impoverished economy."[30] Sandra Steingraber, an ecologist-activist, said that "fracking fits into that category of things that are just inherently bad."[31] But the science and data simply doesn't support these claims.

Take, for instance, environmental fear-mongering about fracking fluid. If green groups are to be believed, energy companies are shooting poisonous chemicals below the earth, polluting the soil and contaminating water.

They're wrong on all counts. As fracking has become more sophisticated, so have the tools used to carry it out. Where once fracking was done with heavy gels, today, far from pumping some corrosive concoction underground, energy producers use formulas that rely heavily on water and sand.

For example, the Cabot Oil & Gas fluid used in Pennsylvania's Marcellus shale is 99.95 percent water and sand, and only .0049 percent chemicals.[32] As for the "chemicals," some are as un-daunting as coffee or walnut shells.[33] So benign are some formulas that Halliburton CEO Dave Lesar,[34] as well as Colorado Governor John Hickenlooper,[35] have recently drunk glasses of fracking fluid.

Claims that the fracking process contaminates groundwater have proven equally ill-founded. Lisa Jackson, the former EPA head, has repeatedly[36] admitted[37] that the scientific data has not yet pointed to a single conclusive or definitive case where groundwater has been contaminated.

Likewise, the Secretary of the U.S. Department of Energy, Ernest Moniz, has spoken out about the environmental benefits of natural gas, saying in 2013 that he had "still not seen any evidence of fracking per se contaminating groundwater."[38]

Numerous credible studies, including from the U.S. Geological Survey, several state governments, the State Review of Oil and Natural Gas Environmental Regulations, Inc., the Massachusetts Institute of Technology, and the U.S. Department of Energy and Ground Water Protection Council have all concluded that evidence supporting a link between fracking and groundwater contamination is simply lacking.[39]

Unfortunately, for some environmental advocates and entrepreneurs, there's a strong financial interest in promoting a deceptive, non-scientific campaign against fracking—one that jeopardizes the incredible promise of American energy.

OUR MISGUIDED POLICY OF PROPPING UP INEFFICIENT ALTERNATIVE ENERGY SOURCES

Right now, renewable energy is neither cost-effective nor capable of meeting America's energy needs. In 2012, wind-, solar-, geothermal- and biomass-generated electricity combined accounted for only 5 percent of all American energy, despite massive taxpayer-funded support propping up these sectors.[40] Furthermore, renewable energy is often two or three times as expensive as more traditional sources.

The profit in green energy comes as much—if not more—from government largesse than from actual market demand for renewable products. So comprehensive are these subsidy programs that it becomes more difficult by the year to get a firm tally on the total amount of taxpayer dollars driven to support these energy sources.

By some estimates, between 1973 and 2012, the Department of Energy and its predecessors alone spent more than $154.7 billion in tax dollars to support clean-energy development—"and has yet to produce a significant energy technology that is commercially viable (i.e., without tax breaks and/or subsidies)" the National Center for Policy Analysis has noted.[41]

Spending on green technology has sharply increased under the Obama administration. A few highlights from the bonanza: In October 2013, the Department of Energy announced a $60 million subsidy program for solar companies[42]—this after the very same agency gave around $8.3 billion in stimulus-era, clean-energy loans, much of which went to failing companies like Solyndra.[43] In 2013, the federal government gave an estimated $7.3 billion in energy tax subsidies for renewables, as well as an additional $4.8 billion in tax credits to support energy efficiency.[44] Altogether, the Department of Energy currently finances at least $32.4 billion in clean-energy loans.[45] In fiscal year 2010, the federal government spent more than $13.65 billion on green-energy subsidies.[46] That list is by no means comprehensive.

Subsidizing green energy isn't just a federal effort, either. At least 29 states have enacted renewable-electricity mandates, and an additional seven have renewable-electricity goals, according to the Institute for Energy Research. That's an expensive strategy. The Heritage Foundation has estimated that such renewable-electricity mandates hike household energy prices by 36 percent, also costing more than a million jobs.[47]

Green-energy companies rightly see abundant, cheap natural gas as their stiffest competition. It's no surprise they're willing to play dirty, using arguments not based in legitimate science to smear fracking and natural gas. Unfortunately, renewable-energy companies have increasingly used their friends in the green, not-for-profit sector to push for energy policies built around these falsehoods.

This corporate agenda hurts America's energy policy, as well as its economy, foreign policy, and the global environment. If the United States truly wants to move toward a cleaner future, it must search for renewable technology that can survive the true test of the market, absent massive taxpayer support. The current approach simply wastes public funds, while also skewing the marketplace and sucking up money that could be put to better use elsewhere.

As the hunt for this elusive viable green technology continues, the United States should make the most of its existing energy resources—

especially natural gas, which can serve as a bridge toward a better environment. Energy production must be safe, but as the history of fracking has demonstrated, technology continues to improve, even more competently ensuring that access to America's oil and gas doesn't compromise its environment or its citizens. Regulation may well play an important role in reinforcing safe and responsible access—but only if it's based in legitimate science, rather than knee-jerk fear-mongering propagated by those who stand to profit from those regulations.

POLICY REFORMS TO IMPROVE OUR ENERGY INFRASTRUCTURE

The policy solution, then, is to eliminate wasteful subsidies that distort the energy market, and instead implement policies that make the most of the clean potential of natural gas and other natural resources. Some specific reforms include:

- Permanently discontinue the production tax credit for wind, which was first enacted in 1992 as a purportedly "temporary" measure and has been repeatedly renewed. Even a one-year extension ends up costing taxpayers $10 billion.[48] This subsidy is so distortionary that wind producers actually profit from selling energy in excess of demand to the utility companies, banking off the ensuing tax credit despite adding no real value to the American energy portfolio.[49]

- Eliminate state-level renewable energy mandates. Many states have mandates that require that all energy sources include a set amount of energy from renewable sources. Consumers in states with these mandates see electricity prices nearly 40 percent higher than their counterparts in states without such requirements.[50]

- End ethanol mandates, which drive up the costs of gas, decrease the miles per gallon vehicles can drive, and can damage car engines.[51] On top of that, because so much corn is being diverted to less efficient use in the energy market, this mandate has also driven up food prices.[52]

- End requirements for use of cellulosic biofuel. Currently, the government has mandated the use of the fuel, which is derived from non-edible plant parts like wood, grass and cornstalks. But in past years, the EPA has demanded that refiners mix in more of this cellulosic biofuel than actually exists in the American commercial marketplace. And when refiners failed at this impossible task of acquiring as much as the federal government demanded, they were forced to fork over millions of dollars for waivers.[53] Though the federal government has scaled back its requirements somewhat, this is counterproductive energy policy that hurts our economy.

- Stop giving taxpayer-backed loan guarantees to renewable energy companies, many of which are not producing a product that meets a genuine market demand. As we have seen, many of these so-called "green energy" loans are awarded to politically-connected firms that end up wasting taxpayer dollars. This is cronyism at its worst.

- On a state level, quit offering tax breaks to attract renewable energy companies. The government shouldn't be picking winners and losers, and by giving these companies preferential treatment, taxpayers are forced to cover more of the state's overall operating costs.

- Approve Keystone XL, TransCanada's proposed $7 billion investment in American infrastructure[54] that would create more than 40,000 jobs.[55] This project has been examined for negative environmental impacts numerous times and found to be safe; moreover, if America refuses to work with Canada to bring this resource to market then Canada will work with another partner, and likely one that won't be as environmentally cautious. America needs to be able to transport oil for the refining process and should approve this common sense private infrastructure project.
- Expedite approval of projects that would allow the United States to export liquefied natural gas. This would stimulate the American economy while also reducing our liberal-democracy allies' dependence on energy from despotic oil titans.

The boom of the past decade has provided a glimpse of the incredible and diverse potential of American energy. But unless our bountiful resources are coupled with sound policy, they will be squandered.

CHAPTER NINE

MAKING TECHNOLOGY WORK FOR WOMEN

BY CARRIE LUKAS

Technology has changed almost every aspect of our lives, yet this omnipresence makes it easy to take for granted. Americans are now accustomed to being surrounded by low-cost technology that just a generation ago would have been fodder for science fiction.

Yet it is important to celebrate how technology is solving once intractable problems and creating new paradigms for work, communication, and education. We also must recognize the important foundations of the free-enterprise system, which make such innovation possible. We want more life-enhancing innovation and technical development, and common sense reforms and public policies can help take us in that direction.

HOW TECHNOLOGY ENRICHES OUR LIVES

Innovation has always played a critical role in creating new opportunities for American women. Time-saving cleaning devices—such as clothes washers, vacuums, dish washers, microwaves—were a critical element of allowing women to take on greater roles in public life. As the burden of housework eased, women could spend more of their time pursuing an education and working outside of their homes.

Today, advances in communication technology have had a similarly revolutionizing effect. And while everyone has benefited from this innovation, and it often seems as though men are more eager to access the latest new gadget and application, women have been uniquely—and in many ways more personally—touched by technologies that provide new paradigms for work, education and communication.

Telecommuting

An estimated 2.8 million Americans (not including those who are self-employed) consider their primary place of work their home. That means that more than 2 percent of employed Americans are working for pay, but work outside of the typical office, factory, shop, or other business environment.[1]

Yet this statistic fails to fully capture the prevalence of telecommuting today. The Telework Research Network estimates that 20 to 30 million people work from home at least one day a week. Telecommuters can be broken into different groups: "15 to 20 million are road warriors / mobile workers; 10 to 15 million are home businesses; 15 to 20 million work at home part time (with about half doing so 1-2 days a week); and about 3 million are based at home full time (including self-employed)."[2] Overwhelmingly, these are positions and situations that could not exist without the technologies—the cell phones, internet, and wireless technologies—that allow us to create a virtual office from just about anywhere in the world.

The many benefits of telecommuting are obvious. The U.S Census Bureau estimates the average American spends 50 minutes each day commuting between work and home. That adds up to more than four extra hours a week that full-time tele-commuters have to work productively, engage with their family and friends, or to otherwise simply enjoy. Telecommuters save money that would otherwise be used on their commute and help unclog our nation's streets and highways, reducing air pollution.[3]

On a personal level, working from home provides millions of Americans with more flexibility to take care of other responsibilities. Instead of waiting until after work, when stores are crowded, the telecommuter can use lunch hour to buy groceries and take care of other chores. At-home workers can start a load of laundry and be there to greet repair men without impacting their work performance.

Businesses also benefit from these new options. Reducing demand for office space cuts down on expenses associated with paying for space and energy. The Independent Women's Forum, the publisher of this book, has operated as a virtual office since 2011. Money that otherwise would have been spent on rent and office utilities is reallocated to programs and put to more productive use. Our staff meets through regular conference calls and stays in constant touch through email and other wireless technologies. The women working at IWF have greater freedom and options for balancing work and family life, and can focus their work during hours that work for both them and the organization. As a result, IWF has been able to attract highly-talented women to become a part of the team.

Technology has played a key role in making this possible.

Communication

When I was a child in the late 1970s, my mother had a regularly scheduled weekly phone call on Sunday afternoons with her mother. I only occasionally held the phone to speak with my grandmother, since the cost of such long distance calls were prohibitive.

Today, although I currently live in Berlin, Germany, and my parents in Virginia, my kids have almost daily conversations with their grandparents. And of course, they do more than talk with them on the phone. We regularly gather for video chats so that my parents can watch their grandchildren in action, see the latest lost tooth and gymnastics trick.

It is hard to assign a dollar value to what this means in terms of enriching our lives, but surely it is significant. Those same technologies that are so critical for giving us new opportunities to work from home also provide almost endless opportunities to interact with others, no matter what the physical distance.

Such technologies not only allow us to keep in touch with existing friends and families, but also to forge new relationships and communities. Consider that as many as one-third of all marriages in the United States last year were of couples who had met their mates online.[4] Social media outlets allow people to find those who share similar interests, whether that's coping with a new disease, a love of science fiction novels, or a desire to travel to East Asia. Technologies' ability to break down the limitations created by physical distance has made our lives infinitely more diverse and rich.

Entertainment and Shopping

Just a few decades ago, Americans were able to watch programming on a handful of television stations, could tune their radio dials in search of the few functioning stations in their area, and could order from the Sears catalog if they wanted something that wasn't available at their local store. Today, our options have grown exponentially, giving us access to a multitude of new entertainment and shopping options at more affordable prices.

Consider that today there are hundreds of legal digital distribution outlets for downloading television programming and movies. There are numerous technologies that allow us to capture programming, so that we can playback events that occurred live but that were inconvenient to our schedules or that we simply want to watch at a different time.

While commentators often lament the vacuousness of much of what one sees on television, they overlook the incredible growth of educational and inspirational content. Where once children's television consisted of Sesame Street, the Brady Bunch, and a handful of (often violent) cartoons on Saturday morning, today there are several channels available on most cable or dish networks geared toward different children's age groups and offering enriching, as well as entertaining, materials. Science shows and history stations give kids and adults the option of learning while being entertained. In addition to these stations, there is an array of educational video series and games available for purchase or download.

Technology has given Americans access to other kinds of products. Ebay famously facilitated the trade of items, through its online auction house, providing new access for collectors and shoppers throughout the world. The Census Bureau estimates that about 5.8 percent of all purchases in 2013 were made online.[5] An estimated 75 million Americans today use the internet to shop, where they can find better deals, more variety, and avoid the hassle of traveling to and from shopping centers. These new shopping options can have particular appeal for those living in more rural areas or who have limitations on their ability to travel, but all Americans benefit from the more robust competition and greater access to goods created by these online technologies and clearing houses.

Political Engagement

Not long ago, getting involved in the political process required taking time out of your schedule to attend a public meeting or write letters to representatives that would slowly make their way to those elected leaders. Today, political participation can take place in front of any computer screen or wireless devise.

As a result, millions of Americans, including millions of women, are getting involved in political debates both on the national and local level. They have new mechanisms for making their opinions known both to policymakers and to their friends and colleagues. Social networks have facilitated political organizing and enabled the growth of bottom-up grassroots efforts like the Tea Party.

While much of this political debate happens virtually, technology has also facilitated the ability of like-minded people to join together in person, helping to organize meetings, rallies and other networking events by putting people instantly in touch. This democratization of the political process has the potential to create a more engaged, informed citizenry and a more inclusive political process.

Education

The ability to access limitless information and to interface with others online has also created tremendous new paradigms for education and job training.

Women dissatisfied with their local public schools for their children have a multitude of new options. Homeschoolers can use online curricula and social networks to link up with other homeschoolers in their community for additional support and social interaction. Parents can use technologies to provide their children with educational materials to supplement their traditional schooling, and increasingly schools themselves utilize such technologies to bring additional resources into their classrooms.

These new capabilities don't solely help women as mothers, but also help them as education consumers themselves. Working women can use after-work hours to take courses online and earn credits toward a degree. At-home learning opportunities eliminate travel time and make it easier for women to put their often limited free time to use. Women enrolling online don't have to consider how their sex, appearance, or age will impact teachers' expectations for them. The anonymity of the online experience can give students the confidence that they will be judged on their merits, which could encourage more women to explore subject matters that have traditionally been dominated by men.

Sadly, many women and girls may forgo or limit their school involvement out of concern for their personal safety. Women living in high crime areas may be discouraged from enrolling at the local night class because it requires them to traverse dangerous neighborhoods and even spend time in potentially dangerous classrooms and campuses. At-home learning opportunities eliminate these concerns and give women a safe space to focus on their own education.

Women are also finding jobs and opportunities to act as educators through these alternative-learning paradigms. Highly-educated women who have dropped out of the workforce to care for children have the potential to find more flexible, at-home work as an online instructor. That means more job opportunities for women, but also a greater supply of qualified teachers that can help the next generation of students.

POLICIES FOR ENCOURAGING MORE INNOVATION

Technological innovation doesn't just happen by accident: Men and women dedicate time and often considerable resources to developing and deploying new technologies. These investments can be safely made because innovators trust that they will be able to bring those technologies to market, recoup the investments that they have made, and return a profit to investors. Yet government should consider how the policy environment can strengthen those protections and encourage more investment in greater innovation.

Intellectual Property Rights and Cyber Security

Big government can be an incredible impediment to economic growth. In fact, this book details many ways that the government gets in the way of economic growth and innovation by distorting the market process through regulation, taxation and government spending that favor a few, politically-connected industries and entities.

Yet the government also plays a key, irreplaceable role in allowing the market to function: The government's ability to protect property rights is at the very core of a market economy and is a necessary precursory to invention and innovation. The Property Rights Alliance, for example, details the relationship between secure property protections and a growing GDP. As shown in the report, "2013 International Property Rights Index," countries that successfully protected property rights, including trademarks, patents and other intellectual materials, have more robust economic growth than those that fail on these important measures.[6]

On one level, this comes as no surprise and can be easily understood: Why work hard to obtain money or possessions if someone can just take them from you? Why invest in improving your home or opening a business if someone can seize those possessions or the return that you get from them?

But in today's economy, property is much more than just money and physical goods: Intellectual property—the right to ideas, inventions, and the content one creates—has increasingly become key. Our understanding of how to properly define and protect intellectual property has had to evolve rapidly to keep up with our increasingly technological world.

In testimony before the House Judiciary Committee's subcommittee on Courts, Intellectual Property and the Internet, Amazon Vice President Paul Misener was humorous at times as he described his company's development from an online bookstore to a leading dealer of digital products.[7] Little more than a decade ago, Amazon was earnestly describing the value of DVDs to its customers, while reassuring them that the VHS was here to stay.

Of course, now, just a few years later, VHSes are as outdated as the telegraph. Why have things changed so dramatically? In part, it's because our robust property protections encourage innovation that allows content providers to work with distributors to sell their products and be fairly compensated. This has enabled new businesses to develop that are specifically designed to facilitate the legal exchange of digital products. It's also why our entertainment options have exploded—we can access an endless array of songs, movies new and old, and high-quality television shows, including some that are created specifically for use among these new online distribution systems.

For such innovation to continue, government needs to prevent the abuse of intellectual property rights through piracy and counterfeiting. There are real ramifications to that kind of theft, just as there is with the theft of physical goods: It drains resources from legal businesses and discourages creativity and the development of new products and content.

It may be tempting to shrug off violations of property rights when it comes to the entertainment industry—what's the big deal with stealing a song or a downloaded movie?—but the consequences are real. Most people working in the entertainment industry aren't Hollywood celebrities making millions. As John McCoskey of the Motion Picture Association of America testified, the entertainment industry consists of about 108,000 businesses across the country (85 percent of which have fewer than 10 employees), which together support nearly 2 million American jobs and $104 billion in taxes.[8]

Intellectual property abuses aren't simply the province of individual hackers and aren't limited to entertainment. For example, India's Supreme Court decided to deny a U.S-based drug company, Novartis AG, a patent for its ground-breaking cancer medication (Glivec), in spite of 40 other countries having recognized the patent and Novartis's right to protect its intellectual property.[9]

This may not sound like a big deal at first read (few are crying over big drug companies losing a little profit), but it has enormous implications for how much people will continue to invest in developing the next round of medical breakthroughs. People may instinctively object to the high costs of many new drugs and treatments (often overlooking the programs designed to help those who cannot afford them gain access), but companies and investors have to recoup the resources spent on the incredibly costly process of bringing a drug to market. Otherwise, new treatments and cures just won't be developed.

The cost of researching, developing, testing, and finally bringing a new drug to market are mind-boggling. While the industry has often used the short-hand that a company must invest $1 billion to bring a new drug to market, more extensive analysis has found that this overlooks much of the cost, by ignoring all of the research and development that goes into those drugs that ultimately cannot be brought to market. Together that makes the estimate closer to $12 billion that companies invest per drug for those that actually end up in the marketplace.[10]

Once a drug has been developed and tested, the costs of using that formula and producing that product are often comparatively negligible. That's why it is all the more important that those entities who have made the real investment is creating that product are the ones who are allowed to sell it, so that they can make up for their investment and use those profits to reinvest in continuing research.

Our increasingly technological world—with so much information and intellectual property stored and exchanged as data over wireless technologies—has opened the door to theft on a grand scale, including from other countries. The Virginia-based cyber security firm, Mandiant, recently released a report detailing the Chinese People's Liberation army's persistent cyber attacks on U.S. corporate entities. The report alleges that since 2006 a single unit has successfully infiltrated "141 companies spanning 20 major industries, from information technology and telecommunications to aerospace and energy," allowing them to steal "large volumes of valuable intellectual property."[11]

The National Security Agency Director, Gen. Keith Alexander, called cybercrime "the greatest transfer of wealth in history."[12] The price tag for all intellectual property theft from U.S. companies is at least $250 billion a year. That's far more than what businesses pay in federal corporate income taxes. This massive lost income means fewer jobs, reduced pay, and a lower standard of living for Americans. It also discourages investment in innovation that is key for increasing our quality of life in the future. Businesses and potential investors today are asking, why pour resources into research and development when that information and innovation may just be stolen?

This vulnerability also has national security implications: The General Accounting Office found that in 2012 federal agencies reported 46,562 cyber security incidents, which "have placed sensitive information at risk, with potentially serious impacts on federal and military operation; critical infrastructure; and confidentiality, integrity, and availability of sensitive government, private sector, and personal information."[13]

In a rare bipartisan move, the Senate is advancing legislation designed to give the federal government more leverage to discourage the practice. The Deter Cyber Theft Act, sponsored by Democrats Carl Levin of Michigan and Jay Rockefeller of West Virginia and Republicans John McCain of Arizona and Tom Coburn of Oklahoma, would require the director of national intelligence to provide an annual report to Congress on the countries engaged in and supporting these activities, the companies and technologies that have been compromised, and the products and services being sold using stolen information. The report would include a watch list of the countries most involved in supporting intellectual property theft, and the president would be charged with holding offending countries accountable, by blocking the importation of products utilizing stolen information created by state-owned enterprises of priority countries.

Such power would be an important step toward discouraging these costly crimes, without giving up the goal of encouraging legitimate international commerce. After all, trade between countries is enriching, and the American people benefit from the ability to buy and sell products worldwide. However, Americans deserve to have their property rights—including their intellectual property rights—protected. Just as our government wouldn't tolerate the seizure of ships transporting our goods to market, it shouldn't tolerate theft that occurs in cyberspace.

This is a major economic issue that deserves ongoing attention. Our government needs to carefully delineate the proper boundaries for its own use of technology and information gathering, and find better ways to protect Americans' intellectual property rights.

Taxes

Like all Americans, technology companies are overtaxed and waste too much time complying with an endlessly complex tax code. Tax reform that simplifies and dramatically lowers the corporate tax rate would be an important way to encourage greater technological innovation.

Yet some technologies have been targeted for additional, specific taxes. Wireless technology, for example, is singled out for a special tax, which makes it one of the classes of goods with the highest levels of taxation.

This fact—that wireless technologies, like tobacco and alcohol, are singled out for extra taxes—may surprise many Americans. Those who believe government shouldn't micromanage people's lives may object to "sin taxes" like those levied on beer and cigarettes, but at least we can understand the logic behind them. Drinking and smoking tend to lead to bad behaviors and outcomes (what economists refer to as "negative externalities") that create costs for society, and that's why government tries to discourage the use of those products. What's the logic behind extra taxes on wireless goods?

After all, most wireless consumers see access to wireless technologies not only as critical to their everyday life (more than 80 percent consider it an essentially service), but as important for increasing their productivity at work (44 percent) and in school (17 percent).[14]

Yet it is this fact—that wireless communications are considered essential—that makes them an attractive taxation vehicle for governments. And, on average, wireless is taxed at a rate of 16.76 percent, which is nearly two-and-a-half times the average state sales tax.[15] Tax rates greatly vary from state to state. Washington state has the highest tax rate, imposing a state and local charge of 18.6 percent in addition to the federal tax of 5.6 percent, for a total of a 24.2 percent sales tax. Oregon (which has no state sales tax in general) imposes a comparatively modest state tax on wireless of 1.79 percent.

The logic behind these special taxes may once have been that wireless services are a luxury, so that a tax on wireless was a way to soak the rich. Perhaps that made some sense years back when only the wealthy used cell phones or had internet service at home. Today, however, Americans at all income levels use wireless technology. Moreover, a growing number of Americans depend exclusively on cell phones, while forgoing a land-line.

Policymakers may also mistakenly lump wireless services in with pure entertainment, like television. But as described previously, wireless technologies are fundamentally about access to information, and much of that information can be critical for climbing up the economic ladder. People use the internet to find job listings and apply for new positions, to educate their children and receive job training.

Having the ability to access that information from home, rather than having to go to a library, school or office place, is particularly important for women, who are more likely to be caring for children or other family members for much of the day. Working mothers who struggle with competing obligations see these technologies as fundamental, so they can pick up their kids at school at 3 pm and still participate in the 4 pm conference call and then complete paperwork after the kids are asleep.

Far from progressive, taxes on wireless technology particularly affect those with tight budgets and who can't afford to pay the extra dollars a month. High taxes contribute to what has been referred to as the "digital divide," which keeps poorer families from having access to the same information that helps educate the middle and upper class.

In fact, when asked if an additional five dollars a month were added to their wireless bill, one-quarter of current wireless users reported in an industry survey that they would "definitely" reduce their wireless service, and two-thirds would either "definitely" reduce or "consider" reducing their plans. Those with lower incomes, African-Americans, Hispanics, and Americans under age 40 were most likely to report having to consider reducing their wireless access due to rising costs.[16]

Rather than seeing wireless services as a vehicle for filling government coffers, policymakers across the country should be lowering these taxes to encourage the use of technology and end these regressive taxes.

There's an old adage that if you want less of something, then tax it. Americans want more, not less, of these life-enhancing technological breakthroughs. Government officials, from Washington, D.C., to the state capitols to the mayors' offices throughout the country, should roll back punitive taxes on these technologies so that more Americans can enjoy the benefits that they bring.

Reforms to Empower Consumers

Another vital, yet often overlooked, method of encouraging greater technological innovation is returning power and resources to individual consumers. When government decides where to allocate resources to encourage the development of new technologies, they consider many factors, including politics. Government bureaucrats consider where a potential grantee is located, whether the workers are unionized, and often the political giving history of key players in the corporation. That's why we so frequently hear that companies who were awarded government grants also have political connections, and then they turn out to under-deliver or, in many cases, not deliver at all.

Consumers tend to be much better stewards of resources: They use their hard-earned dollars to buy technologies and other products that they believe provide the best value to their lives. As a result, when money flows from individuals, companies with the most innovative, useful technologies are likely to end up with more resources and be better able to invest in developing and bringing to market new breakthroughs.

Consider what this might mean in the education sector. Right now, the average public school student will have more than $100,000 invested in his or her education between kindergarten and graduating high school. Most of that money flows through the traditional public school model, which—while making some progress toward incorporating new technologies and applications into their learning programs—has been extremely slow to adapt and innovate. Imagine if parents controlled more of these resources and could select from a variety of schools and education providers: Entrepreneurs would have tremendous incentive to find solutions that work, and those innovations would create new learning opportunities for Americans at every stage of life.

Policymakers should seek to get out of the way of technological innovation, and stop funding specific entities or technologies that ultimately create an uneven playing field, thereby making it more difficult for startup technologies to emerge. By returning more resources to individual Americans, lawmakers can help encourage the next generation of life-enhancing innovation that can change our society in ways that we can't yet imagine.

CHAPTER TEN

A SAFETY NET THAT EMPOWERS, NOT ENABLES

BY PATRICE J. LEE

Opportunity makes possible the hopes and dreams of Americans. Sometimes, however, disaster strikes or hardship hits. When this happens, Americans want people to have the support they need to rebuild their lives. The task of lifting up those in need shouldn't fall to government alone. Family, friends, and community members working together can form a solid network of support that, along with judiciously applied help from government, enables people to become independent again and lead satisfying lives.

Yet sadly, today, that conception of the safety net is at risk. Government has become more and more inefficient, and in some cases ineffective because it's weighed down by bureaucracy, duplication of efforts, and a lack of accountability. Government programs have also crowded out private giving, which tends to be better suited to the local needs of communities and can best help encourage self-help. Alarmingly, many government poverty-alleviation policies have fostered dependence on government and discouraged family formation and the acquiring of education and work experience that are crucial to long-term independence.

Reform of our social safety net is overdue. When we think about reforming our government's safety net programs, we should be inspired by this vision for society:

We want the unemployment rate falling to new lows even as more Americans enter the workforce. We want there to be multiple jobs for every applicant and full employment for those who want to work. We want the rolls of those on food stamps and receiving welfare to decline. We want people in need to receive the unemployment assistance and other income support they need, but to be encouraged to get back on their feet so they can support themselves again as soon as it is feasible to do so. We want there to be a robust network of support groups—food banks and homeless shelters. It is important to do more than just meet basic needs. We should also foster the attitudes and skills that lead to self-reliance and success.

This is our vision for the future. It's hopeful, attainable, and it will breathe new life into the ideal of the American Dream.

GOOD INTENTIONS, BAD RESULTS

Fifty years ago, when President Lyndon B. Johnson declared an "unconditional war on poverty," he likely had a similar vision and hoped that his programs could achieve it.

Unfortunately, our current reality and the record of his policies show that we are still very far from realizing this vision. In fact, today we have a growing problem of government dependency and too many Americans who don't believe the American Dream applies to them. This is due in part to ill-advised policies that—though well-intentioned—have served to enable lasting reliance on government, rather than providing temporary assistance while encouraging long-term independence.

Statistics tell the story about an America where opportunity has waned and the safety net has grown to become a trap that ensnares all too many Americans in a life of permanent dependence. One in seven Americans (some 46.5 million people) lives below the official poverty line[1] and receives food stamps. The number of food stamp recipients has actually increased by 50 percent since January of 2009.[2] The current effective unemployment rate, which includes those who can't find work and those working less than they desire, stands at 15 percent.[3] Fewer Americans are currently in the workforce—63 percent— than at any time since the Bureau of Labor Statistics began collecting data. In fact, 13 percent of 18-29 year old women are sitting at home right now with no jobs and are discouraged from even looking for work.[4] And speaking of home, on any given night there are reportedly 610,000 people with no place to call home. Of that number, more than one third are in families, and 18 percent are considered chronically homeless.[5]

These distressing numbers come in spite of government's massive investment in alleviating poverty through programmatic spending. Entitlement spending accounts for nearly two-thirds of federal spending today, up from less than a third in 1960.[6] Over the last 50 years, the U.S. government has spent $20.7 trillion on over 80 welfare programs that provide food, cash, housing, medical care, and educational and social services to poor and low-income Americans. Yet, the poverty rate has only fallen marginally to 15 percent from 19 percent in 1964 when President Johnson declared the War on Poverty.

Most Americans agree that there is a minimum of food, shelter, and clothing provisions our country should make available for the truly indigent. The federal government devotes roughly one-sixth of its spending to ten major, means-tested programs and tax credits that do so.[7] These programs constitute our nation's primary, government-provided social safety net, intended to catch Americans who fall on difficult circumstances and to prevent them from suffering from deprivation. However, what was meant as a temporary springboard has become a sticky spider web for many Americans, trapping them in a lifestyle that penalizes them for trying to get free.

We can do better.

We must embrace reforms to government programs that empower beneficiaries to take control of their own futures and achieve success. The goal of our safety net programs should be to reduce poverty and help more people live flourishing lives by offering temporary support to those who can get back on their feet, and by targeting long-term aid to only those who truly need it.

THE FAMILY: THE FIRST, BEST SAFETY NET

Before discussing the government programs that exist to help those in need, it is worth considering what has throughout the history of civilization been the first-line safety net for people needing help: the family. Family, based on marriage, is the most basic unit of society. Families are the place where individuals typically first gather their sense of belonging, self-worth, value systems, and emotional support. Families are also a sustainable source of support for children and the elderly, as well as those who fall on hard times.

No family is perfect, but this basic fact remains as true today as it was centuries ago: Two people who marry and raise their children together best ensure the current and future welfare of those children and society more broadly.

One of the most unfortunate consequences of government welfare programs has been their damaging effect on the family, discouraging the development and maintenance of two-parent households, especially among those with low-incomes. In fact, government programs have created perverse incentives that reward single-parent households at the expense of the financial security, educational success, and social stability that two-parent households create. And surely this has contributed to the dramatic decline in the prevalence of married family households. In 1963, seven percent of American children were born out of wedlock. Today, that number is 41 percent.[8] Poor and working-class Americans are much less likely to get married and stay married, and their kids are more likely to be exposed to family turmoil and single parenthood.

This trend is harmful to children. Living with a single parent can produce negative behavior issues such as "acting out," skipping school, or dropping out of high school, and to a smaller extent cognitive issues, such as academic performance.[9] Harvard economist Raj Chetty and his colleagues found that when it comes to upward economic mobility for poor kids, "the strongest and most robust predictor [of mobility] is the fraction of children living with single parents."[10] Furthermore, communities with fewer single parent households have been found to be more conducive to helping young minds develop and to go on to lead productive lives.

Any fruitful discussion about poverty stabilization in this country cannot ignore the complex problems associated with single-parent households. A marriage license is not a cure-all. However, by changing the incentives and cultural attitudes around marriage, we can change behavior. Eventually, norms will follow.

RESCUING PEOPLE FROM A DIET OF DEPENDENCE

Food is one of the most basic needs. Without adequate nutrition, a student will struggle to concentrate on her lessons whether she is in the first grade or a college senior. Nobody should go hungry, but similarly nobody should rely on the government for sustenance long-term, unless there are truly extenuating circumstances.

An alarming number of Americans have come to do just that. Food stamp usage has risen dramatically in recent years. Last year, 47 million— that's nearly one out of every seven Americans—were served by the Supplemental Nutrition Assistance Program (SNAP), formerly known as the Food Stamp program.[11] SNAP provides an average of $133.08 per month in federally-funded food assistance for people living in the U.S. with no or low income. Food stamp spending has grown rapidly in recent years, from $17 billion in 2000 to $79.9 billion in Fiscal Year 2013.[12]

The provision of food support is fraught with abuse, mismanagement, lack of oversight and duplication of efforts. By implementing reforms that minimize waste and boost individual personal responsibility, we can empower more Americans to become independent from government largess while still helping those in need. There are several ways policymakers can improve our food stamp and welfare programs in ways that do not promote dependence:

- **Reform Incentives for State Governments to Encourage Independence**: Currently, state governments receive automatic increases in funding for SNAP benefits when they increase the number of recipients on their rolls. We need to change this formulation so that states are not encouraged to endlessly expand the pool of those dependent on this government handout. The federal government should instead cap SNAP spending and give each state a block grant that is set to increase at no more than inflation. Caps can be made flexible in the event of a severe economic decline, but should not be an excuse for another permanent expansion of the program. Analysts estimate that such an approach would save the federal government roughly $150 billion over the next decade.[13]

- **States Should Target Aid to Those Truly in Need**: The current Administration has promoted "broad-based categorical eligibility," a loophole that permits states to add a person or household to the food assistance rolls without income and asset tests for eligibility. For someone to be eligible for SNAP, they need only receive cash aid or any other means-tested services. So for example, a middle-class family with one earner who becomes temporarily unemployed can receive $668 per month in food stamps even if the family has $200,000 in cash sitting in the bank. According to an estimate by the House of Representatives Committee on the Budget, closing this loophole would save taxpayers $14.3 billion over the next 10 years.[14]

- **Couple Food Stamp Benefits with Work Activation Programs**: A strong economy that is generating jobs is the strongest ally in efforts against poverty. However, as we wait for the economy to return to full strength, we can require able-bodied, food-stamp recipients to work, prepare for work, or actively seek work as a condition to receiving aid. A work activation program could also increase the hours of work among those who are employed part-time. This is truly a transformative solution that boosts an individual's professional development and economic independence.

Remember, those who receive unemployment benefits must complete weekly reports with names and contact information of several jobs for which they have applied. This should be no different for the men and women receiving food stamps. There are 10.5 million food stamp households that contain able-bodied, non-elderly adults, yet 5.5 million performed zero work during the month.[15] We should be encouraging work for those who are able through all safety net programs.

REFORMING WELFARE—AGAIN

Part of the success of welfare reform in the 1990s was that it alleviated poverty and reduced dependency by turning so-called welfare moms into productive workers. The results were immediate as employment of single mothers surged, caseloads of welfare recipients dropped by half in just four years, and child poverty dropped at an unprecedented rate. In the same time period, the poverty rate of children of single mothers dropped from 50.3 percent in 1995 to 39.8 percent in 2001.[16]

Recently President Barack Obama instituted policies to gut welfare reform by jettisoning its work requirements. In 2012, the Administration released directives that permitted states to waive the work requirement in welfare law. In place of the legislated work requirements, the administration has stated, it will design its own "work" systems without congressional involvement or consent. Under the new directives, only about 1.8 percent of a state's Temporary Assistance for Needy Families (TANF) caseloads need to be gainfully employed each month.[17] That lowers the bar to the point where states can stumble over it without trying. As the economy improves, most states will naturally see recipients fall off their rolls. Keeping Americans on welfare rolls does nothing for Americans, but keeps them beholden to government handouts.

We have work to do. We need to reverse these new directives and tighten work requirements. The potential for a decline in welfare recipients is there. This would not only help taxpayers and ease burdens on federal and state budgets, but most importantly it would change the trajectory of so many Americans who currently feel left out of the American Dream. Instead of receiving handouts, they'd be earning a paycheck and beginning their ascent up the economic ladder.

Here are two other suggestions to improve our welfare system to make it work for those in need:

- **Discourage the Use of Drugs Among Welfare Recipients**: Drug use among welfare recipients is not a myth, as studies show that 21 percent of mothers receiving welfare have reported using illegal drugs in the prior year.[18] Because self-reporting of illegal drug use is likely lower than actual use, these numbers are an understatement of the actual prevalence of drug abuse among welfare recipients. Taxpayer dollars should not go to facilitate a drug habit. This policy is not meant to coldly punish those with substance abuse problems, but simply recognizes that money provided to those addicted to drugs can make their problems worse. Recipients of aid should be required to take and pass drug testing. Those who fail drug testing should be encouraged to use programs to help overcome addiction and transition out of that destructive life-style.
- **Provide Non-cash Assistance**: The government can and should seek to alleviate some of the most difficult obstacles for welfare recipients who are trying to rejoin

the working world, such as the lack of child care or transportation. Child care assistance is a key element of welfare reform because many low-income working parents, including most single mothers leaving welfare for work, need help paying for child care.

The family unit has filled that role in past generations as grandparents living in the household would watch young ones. In many homes today, however, that is no longer a possibility as older generations are less likely to live in close proximity or are unavailable for other reasons. As the costs of child care grows, it is increasingly more cost-effective for some parents to stay at home and raise a child rather than work at entry-level, low-paying jobs. Stipends that help offset the costs of child care while a parent is at work, seeking employment, or gaining new skills give them freedom to focus on their employment and career success. It was in fact an integral part of 1996 welfare reform.

Policymakers need to keep this key point in mind: When the financial payoff from government safety-net programs is greater than what one can earn in the marketplace, welfare recipients have an incentive to continue receiving benefits and not join the workforce. According to the Cato Institute, welfare benefits outpace the income that most recipients can expect to earn from an entry-level position. Welfare pays recipients more than a minimum wage job in 35 states, and in 13 states it pays more than $15 per hour. In 39 states, welfare pays more than the starting wage for a secretary and in 11 states, it pays more than the average pre-tax first year wage for a teacher. Hawaii, the District of Columbia, and Massachusetts provide the highest levels of benefits providing the pre-tax equivalent of $60,590, $50,820, and $50,540 respectively.[19] That's greater than an entry-level computer programmer.

Federal policy can shift the balance between welfare and work, both by limiting access to benefits and helping to increase the income of those rejoining the workforce (through pro-growth economic policies or other methods, such as through the Earned Income Tax Credit) so that employment becomes more attractive.

MEDICAID: LET'S REMOVE PERVERSE INCENTIVES AND EMPOWER PATIENTS

There's no better place to find duplicative federal spending than in health care. We're not just talking about overspending on extra scalpels or over reporting doctor's visits. We're talking about a system that costs states and the federal government billions and all too often fails those it is supposed to help.

As discussed in chapter three, America needs to rethink its approach to the provision of health care and put patients and consumers in charge. This would control costs and create a more efficient, effective health care system.

It is essential that Medicaid, a pillar of America's overall safety net program for the poor, be reformed. This joint federal-state program provides health coverage for more than 60 million indigent Americans, including children, pregnant women, parents, seniors and individuals with disabilities.[20] States establish and administer their own Medicaid programs. They get to determine the type, amount, duration, and scope of services but are required by law to cover certain "mandatory benefits," and can choose to provide other "optional benefits," including prescription drugs. States receive federal matching funds to provide these benefits. The open-ended nature of Medicaid federal funding encourages states to increase spending. And since the grants are distributed poorly, federal dollars are not flowing to the states with greater concentrations of people in need.

One solution would be for the federal government to give each state an annual block grant to achieve the goals of providing health care for the poor and disabled. That would remove the perverse incentive of trying to qualify for more federal funds and give states more flexibility to tailor their programs to meet local needs.

As discussed in more detail in chapter three, those reforming Medicaid should also focus on empowering patients in this community so that they can buy health insurance coverage that meets their needs and improves their access to care, and not as a separate (and often inferior class) of Medicaid recipients. Importantly, as states consider reforming health insurance support programs such as Medicaid, they should also keep in mind how those programs phase out as a recipient enters the workforce: We do not want the fear of losing access to health insurance subsidies to discourage people from getting a job.

UNEMPLOYMENT: A SAFETY NET, NOT A WAY OF LIFE

Sometimes people find themselves unemployed through no fault of their own. Often those reasons stem from downturns in the economy that force employers to make the difficult decision of laying off workers. It may be that business is too slow to warrant the expense of a position, or larger structural issues may be at play.

Unemployment insurance (UI) provides an important safety net for individuals who find themselves between jobs. While it doesn't replace one's full paycheck, it does deliver cash benefits as well as trainings that can be helpful as a person transitions from one role to another.

Problems arise, however, with longer-term unemployment. Benefits can discourage workers from expanding their job search, exploring relocation, or accepting a job outside of their field, which can contribute to an extended period of unemployment. Long-term unemployment in itself is incredibly destructive for an individual's job prospects as skills, networks, and job histories fade, making that worker a less desirable potential hire.

The typical unemployed worker spends about 32 minutes a day looking for a new job. Workers eligible for UI benefits spend about 20 minutes looking for work during their 15th week of unemployment, but that triples to more than 70 minutes when their benefits are about to end. Unsurprisingly, it takes workers with UI longer to find new jobs. [21] Though not ideal, beneficiaries learn to adjust to this new income level, which may not be dramatically lower than when they were employed if unemployment is coupled with other new benefits, such as food assistance. It is understandable that some people may decide to continue receiving aid rather than taking a less desirable job.

Today, people can receive UI benefits for up to 99 weeks. Reducing that time period may be painful for unemployed workers, but is the "tough love" that they need to encourage them to reconsider their job search, look beyond their current city or state, or take a pay cut to find work in a different field.

While making this change, policymakers should boost requirements and opportunities for trainings, courses, and certifications as a condition for UI benefits that help smooth the transition and fill in the skills gaps. For example, AEI's Robert Stein has proposed innovative programs, such as relocation assistance for the long-term unemployed so that someone stuck in an area with high unemployment can move to an area with better job prospects and incentive programs to encourage employers to hire the long-term unemployed by reducing their effective wage. These are reforms that encourage workers to take ownership of their future and to encourage initiative, rather than simply provide a band-aid for their immediate financial woes.

SOCIAL SECURITY DISABILITY INSURANCE: FOR THE DISABLED ONLY

Welfare, food stamps, and unemployment benefits are not the only federal assistance programs in need of reform. Social security disability income (SSDI) is dispensed to those who are injured or who suffer from illnesses that preclude them from working. SSDI often goes overlooked, but is an easy place to find abuse, exploitation, and waste.

According to the Social Security Administration, SSDI was paid to 11 million Americans in December 2013. Approximately 82 percent of payments went to disabled workers. Men accounted for slightly more than half of all recipients. On average these workers received a monthly benefit of $1,146.[22]

The challenge with this program is that once the benefit is granted, it may be an indefinite income source. Once an ill worker begins receiving disability payments, he or she may never recover enough (or claim to be fit enough) to return to work. That is in part due to the nature of illnesses that qualify for help. In recent years, the biggest increases in disability claims have been for "musculoskeletal" problems and mental disorders (including mood disorders). It is difficult, if not impossible, for a health professional to ascertain whether a patient is suffering from back pain or depression, or when those symptoms end. This leaves this program open to the potential for massive abuse.

Senator Tom Coburn investigated three hundred cases of Americans who had been awarded disability benefits and found that more than one quarter of them provided insufficient, contradictory, or incomplete evidence. What this signals is that these could very well be fraudulent claims of injury from those seeking permanent "free money" from the government.

In addition, SSDI is often tied to other forms of government assistance, such as health benefits. And many disability recipients matriculate from the disability roll right onto the retirement benefits roll. In 2011, more than half of those whose disability benefits ceased did not do so because they returned to work, but because they had reached full retirement age and now qualified for traditional Social Security benefits. Medical improvement only accounted for 3.6 percent, and 6.1 percent returned to work.[23]

Given that the average age for disabled workers is 53, it's easy to see how one has a strong incentive to stay on disability, along with other benefits, until retirement age arrives. If the economy is not generating enough employment for workers, and older workers in particular, then all of these benefits with no accountability or restrictions may encourage a lifestyle of government dependency.

STREAMLINING PROGRAMS

The U.S. government could save tens of billions of dollars a year by streamlining the federal bureaucracy related to income assistance and the safety net. Duplication makes it easy for recipients to game the system at the expense of taxpayers.

The Government Accountability Office releases an annual report of a wide range of federal programs, agencies, offices and initiatives to identify where the government is duplicating its goals or activities. For example, the GAO recommends that Congress consider passing legislation to prevent individuals from collecting both full disability insurance benefits and unemployment insurance benefits that cover the same period. This could save $1.2 billion over 10 years in the Social Security Disability Insurance program, according to the Congressional Budget Office.[24] Also, by enhancing information sharing between state and federal agencies, the Department of Labor could identify potentially improper payments, including inappropriate overlapping payments between federal employees' compensation and unemployment insurance administered by the states.

And policymakers ought to consider going beyond just consolidating overlapping programs, and take an entirely new approach to assisting those with low incomes. Instead of myriad programs designed to provide different forms of aid and income support, government could simply provide cash-assistance to those with low-incomes and permit them to make decisions for themselves about how to use those resources. This would eliminate much of the waste, red tape, and duplication that plague the current system.

And it just might work toward encouraging better stewardship of resources and greater initiative toward self-improvement. The Ugandan government tried an experiment where it offered young adults the chance to band together, submit a proposal and receive a big sum — equivalent to a year's income per person — with no follow-up. The idea was to encourage the young workers to shift from agriculture and casual labor into manufacturing and service trades. Participants were much more likely to enroll in skills training after receiving this one-time sum, and it increased the labor supply. Their earnings increased on two- and four-year horizons, especially among women, who after four years had average earnings 84 percent higher than women who had not participated in this program. All in all, the annualized return on the "investment" of the cash transfer worked out to a whopping 40 percent.[25]

Of all of the solutions discussed, this is likely the most controversial, but also the most liberating and respectful of an individual's right to choose how to best address their short-term and long-term needs. If we truly believe in an individual's desire to lift themselves from poverty, then we must pursue responsible policies that empower them to do so. Piling as many people into the complicated, bureaucratic social safety net only weighs it down and makes it a comfortable place, reducing the desire for each person to climb out. Narrowing the net and ensuring it truly is a spring board can propel each person to get out and land on their feet.

ACTIVE CITIZENS WHO OWN THEIR FUTURES

There are common threads among the proposals and plans explored in this chapter. We need common sense reforms that tighten eligibility requirements for government subsidies, encourage work, focus aid on those truly in need, and encourage states to help people get off of assistance rather than increase their welfare rolls. In all of these cases, the goal is to move aid recipients from a passive role of receiving benefits to an active role in owning their future.

There is an entitlement mentality that expects a certain provision of benefits by government, no questions asked. These reforms are not about eliminating the social safety net, but changing that mentality by ensuring that the ones who benefit from these programs are those truly in need of them.

Poverty-alleviation policies have done wonders in keeping the poor beholden to government. They have succeeded in fostering an unhealthy independence that robs Americans of the opportunity to fulfill their God-given potential. Yet they have not succeeded in giving these Americans access to the American Dream of self-improvement and earned prosperity. As we consider how to reform these programs, that should be our driving goal.

CHAPTER ELEVEN

RETIREMENT AND SAVING FOR THE FUTURE

BY CARRIE LUKAS

We want people to be able to retire with the security that they have the financial resources to live comfortably and will have the resources to meet their needs in the years ahead. We also want a system that helps people save for retirement during their working lives, but saving for retirement also can't become such a burden that it prevents people from making needed investments in other priorities.

Our public pension systems provide an important foundation for Americans' retirement security. However, they have very real limitations and impose very real costs on working Americans. Worse, they too often face significant financial problems, which means that they are unlikely to deliver the benefits that are currently being promised in the future, and could create real hardship for the next generation of workers who will have to shoulder the burden of propping up these underfunded systems.

We need to reform these programs so that they are sustainable, provide adequately for people at retirement, and do not become a burden that depresses needed economic growth and innovation in the years to come. Moreover, we need to reform our treatment of savings vehicles to encourage more individual saving both for retirement and for other important needs.

OUR AILING PUBLIC PENSION SYSTEMS

Our government-run public pension systems are supposed to be an important aspect of Americans' overall retirement savings plan. Indeed, Social Security provides a majority of retirees with a majority of their retirement income, and payments into Social Security are the largest tax the average working American pays each year. In addition to Social Security, governments at all levels operate pension systems for some government workers. Given that today government employs about 16 percent of workers, this ends up playing a significant role in the country's overall retirement security.[1]

Yet sadly, while these programs are critical, they often have significant financial problems. Most public pension systems are seriously underfunded, which means that they may be unable to pay all benefits that have been promised to current retirees and to the workers currently contributing to the program today, who expect future benefits. That also means that these underfunded programs are a significant liability for taxpayers, since governments will turn to current and future taxpayers to pay more so they can make good on promised benefits.

Social Security

Today, nearly 40 million Americans over age 65 receive Social Security's retirement benefits. The average retired worker receives a monthly benefit of $1,251.36.[2] For two-thirds of seniors, Social Security accounts for more than half of monthly income, and for more than one-third (35 percent) of seniors, Social Security accounts for more than 90 percent of monthly income.[3]

This means that Social Security is a critical part of America's financial security system. Unfortunately, the program itself faces significant financial problems of its own, because it relies on what is known as a pay-as-you-go system. That means that taxes collected today are used immediately to fund benefits to current retirees. Nothing is saved for the future.

The stability of such a structure depends on having more people paying in to the system than people taking benefits out of the system. That was the case when Social Security was designed. In 1940, there were more than 150 workers paying taxes to Social Security for each Social Security beneficiary. By 1960, there were five workers per beneficiary. Today, there are less than three workers paying in for each person taking retirement benefits out.[4]

That ratio is going to continue to get worse because of important demographic trends, such as our low birth rate, people living longer, and growth in the retiree population. This means that right now, when Social Security owes a retiree a monthly check for $1200, the Social Security Administration (SSA) needs to collect about $400 each from three workers. That's a significant cost for the average American worker today. As the number of workers per retiree falls, each worker will have to pay significantly more to support those benefits. By 2020, the SSA estimates there will be just 2.1 workers per retiree, so that $1200 monthly benefit would essentially have to be split between two workers—a very significant burden for the shrinking pool of working Americans.

Today, Social Security payroll taxes already aren't generating enough money to cover benefits. This is a problem that will continue to get worse in years ahead, and taxes will have to rise considerably if the government is to make good on current promises.

Social Security's financial problems are just one of the system's flaws. Social Security also doesn't provide a very good deal for many Americans— and the outcomes from Social Security are often simply unfair. How much one receives from Social Security largely depends on how long one lives. Some people pay into Social Security through their working lives, die at age 65 before retiring, and receive nothing back from Social Security in spite of years of contributions. Since those with lower incomes also have lower life expectancies, this can particularly harm the poor.

Social Security also rewards some family structures over others. A married woman with a working husband can work for years and pay into Social Security, but end up no better off than if she had not worked at all.

As policymakers consider how to reform Social Security, they should try to do more than just get Social Security's books to balance. They need to try to create a system that is equitable and helps Americans become a nation of savers.

What About the Trust Fund?

The SSA has a Social Security Trust Fund with about $2.5 trillion in assets to fund retirement benefits. Since 2010, payroll taxes collected to fund Social Security haven't been enough to cover all benefit payments, so SSA has been withdrawing assets from the Trust Fund to make up for the shortfall (which was about $55 billion in 2012).[5]

The existence of such a Trust Fund is great news for taxpayers, right?

Not exactly. When SSA goes to cash in the bonds in the Trust Fund, the general treasury has to come up with the money to pay SSA back. That means that it has to take the money out of the general budget or issue new debt. In other words, the Trust Fund may be an asset for SSA, but it's a liability for American taxpayers. When SSA cashes in trust fund assets, *you* have to pay the bill.

This means that in addition to paying 12.4 percent of income to payroll taxes (which is split between employer and employee), in future years, Social Security will also consume a growing share of Americans' incomes taxes. This will put additional pressure on our already stretched budget and increase our deficit and national debt. Congress will have less money to spend on other priorities—whether that's fighting a war or addressing natural disasters—since tens of billions, and then ultimately hundreds of billions, will have to go to paying back Social Security's Trust Fund.

Social Security's Trust Fund is expected to run out in 19 years. At that point, payroll taxes would cover about three-quarters of promised benefits.[6] So if nothing is done to reform Social Security, future beneficiaries will see their checks slashed, or Congress will have to raise payroll taxes on workers dramatically. Such payroll tax increases could have a devastating impact on the economy, reducing the budgets of families with children and making employment scarcer.

Clearly, timely action is needed to address Social Security's present financial difficulties before we reach such a crisis.

Other Public Pensions

Most other government pension systems are also defined benefit systems, which mean that workers pay in a set amount while working and then are owed a defined benefit when they retire, regardless of what assets are in the system or how the money was invested in the interim.

Unlike Social Security, state and local public pension systems are supposed to be pre-funded, meaning that unlike Social Security's pay-as-you-go system, contributions collected for state and local pension system are supposed to be held in a fund, so that assets can accrue over time and then be used to fund the benefits for retirees.

However, unfortunately, many public pension systems are inadequately funded, which means that the system's assets and expected income are not enough to cover the benefits that have been promised from the system. Economists and policymakers debate the best way to value the assets and liabilities in pension systems, but as the Congressional Budget Office reports, a study of 126 state and local pension plans showed that together, they have between a $0.7 trillion and a $3.0 trillion shortfall.[7]

Part of the problem is that over the years, many government officials have found it politically advantageous to increase compensation packages for their state and local government workers, who are heavily unionized and often an important voting block. Augmenting benefit packages is a tempting route to take, because it impacts taxpayers in the future, rather than current taxpayers. Thus they are able to offer a considerable benefit to some constituents without considering costs, since taxpayers are unlikely to focus on how such benefit increases will affect tax bills years down the road.

Changing this dynamic—which can effectively allow public workers and union workers to collude to fleece taxpayers—is an important aspect of lasting public pension reform.

CREATING SUSTAINABLE GOVERNMENT PENSION SYSTEMS

Policymakers need to consider ways to reform our public retirement systems so they are financially sound, provide real security, and are a sensible investment for Americans. To the extent possible, policymakers should seek to phase in changes so that people have time to adjust their plans and prepare for retirement.

Social Security Reform

Instead of allowing Social Security to continue on its current path of burdening American taxpayers, adding to our national debt, and ultimately disappointing beneficiaries, Congress should make prudent changes to bring Social Security's costs down today and ensure that they grow more slowly in the future. There are many ways to reduce Social Security's costs. For example, Congress could consider raising the age of eligibility for Social Security for future retirees.

In 1940, a man who reached age 65 was expected to live an average of 12.7 more years, and a woman was expected to live 14.7 years. As of 2007, the 65-year-old man expected to live 17.2 years and the woman 19.9.[8] That's four and a half more years of payments for the man and five years more of payments for the woman. Those extra checks add up.

Medical breakthroughs and advances in safety technologies mean that we can expect average lifespans to continue to increase. That's great news for all of us who can expect to live longer and healthier, but it's bad news for Social Security's finances. When Social Security was envisioned, no one expected millions of Americans to receive government retirement checks for thirty, or even forty, years. Yet that's increasingly the case today, and will become more commonplace as life expectancies rise.

Social Security's age of eligibility should be raised gradually and then indexed to life expectancy to help bring costs down and return the system to its original intentions.

Policymakers should also review how cost of living increases are calculated. For example, as the Mercatus Center's Charles Blahous explains:

[Social Security's] basic benefit formula is indexed to growth in the Average Wage Index (AWI), which tends over time to rise faster than price inflation. As a result, real per-capita Social Security benefits are already rising substantially under current law. Partisans sometimes apply the misleading terminology of "benefit cuts" to proposals to adjust benefit growth to sustainable rates, but the reality is that under virtually any plausible reform scenario, benefits will still rise in real terms relative to what seniors receive today.[9]

This is an important point to keep in mind. Under current law, people are receiving more generous Social Security benefits, in real dollar terms, than beneficiaries were a generation ago, and the value of Social Security benefits are expected to increase for future retirees. As Blahous goes on to note, such increasing benefits sound wonderful, until one also considers the costs of paying for those benefits. Given that Social Security's finances are already out of balance and the per-worker cost of providing Social Security benefits is climbing rapidly, Congress ought to consider changes to how benefits are calculated so that rather than promising more generous retirement benefits to future workers (which the federal government will be unable to fully pay for under current law), future retirees benefits are comparable to those received today.

Congress should also consider explicit reductions in benefits that are paid out to high-income retirees. Social Security isn't meant to be a welfare program, and the benefits that are received are supposed to bear a relationship to taxes paid in during one's working life. However, given Social Security's bleak prospects, changes have to be made, and those seniors with the highest incomes will be better able to withstand reduced benefit payments. It may not be fair, but it may be necessary.

The Social Security System Americans Deserve

Reducing Social Security's future costs will be necessary to avert economic disaster and ensure that the program is sustainable in the long-term. But these changes alone aren't enough. And in fact, while needed, such changes will exacerbate some of Social Security's other flaws.

For example, reductions in the growth of future benefits will make the system a worse deal for program participants. Those who die before or immediately after retirement age will still have nothing to show for a lifetime of contributions to Social Security. How much someone receives from Social Security will still be influenced by marital status and life expectancy, creating unfair outcomes for many.

That's why simply making the current Social Security system sustainable shouldn't be the only goal of reform. Ultimately, policymakers should consider how to move toward a system that allows people to save and invest on their own. A defined contribution system, which consists of personally-owned retirement accounts, for example, would allow people to put money away for their own retirement, and those assets would grow during their working lives. That account would be someone's personal property and could be passed on at death or divided in the event of a divorce.

Such a system would be much more fair in terms of the treatment of individuals: Those who work longer would contribute more and would have more assets at the end; those who die before reaching retirement would at least be able to pass a nest egg on to their love ones, rather than forfeiting a lifetime of savings.

There are many ways to incorporate a system of personal accounts into Social Security while maintaining a basic safety net (to make sure that, regardless of the performance of the financial markets, everyone eligible for Social Security receives income support that keeps them out of poverty). Many of these proposals are more progressive, guaranteeing greater benefits for those with lower incomes while reducing promised payouts for wealthier cohorts.[10] While policymakers address Social Security's immediate financial challenges, they should also consider how to turn this often-arbitrary pay-as-you-go system into a system that gives the American people ownership of their retirement assets.

Why Not Raise the Income Cap on Social Security Payroll Taxes?

Americans currently pay a 12.4 percent Social Security payroll tax on the first $117,000 they earn.[11] Social Security's benefit payments are also based on taxes paid in, so millionaires receive the same Social Security benefit as someone who made just the earnings cap throughout their lives.

Some propose raising, or even eliminating, the income cap so workers pay payroll taxes on more (or all) of what they earn. Yet as The Cato Institute's Michael Tanner explains, eliminating the cap would give the U.S. one of the highest marginal tax rates in the world, and these high taxes would bring down our GDP and cost more than a million jobs.[12] And unless Social Security's benefit formula was radically changed, eliminating the cap would only put off Social Security's financial crisis by about seven years.

We already have too-high taxes on work that are hindering economic mobility for young workers. We should fix Social Security without adding more of a burden to those working today.

Other Public Pension Reforms

Similarly, policymakers need to pursue changes to state and local pension systems to bring them into better financial balance. This should start with reducing benefit promises made to new workers—which will at least help by no longer adding to the systems' unfunded liabilities. Governments should also consider legal ways to gradually reduce obligations and require higher contributions from workers to fund their future benefits. Some states have moved to incorporate a defined contribution system for new employees to offset reductions in defined benefit plans, and to ensure more stable financing moving forward. That's an important transition to make.

A detailed report by Patrick McGuinn of the Brookings Institute examines how different states have proceeded with pension reform, focusing on the experience of four states: Utah, Rhode Island, New Jersey and Illinois.[13] Some states have been able to enact more comprehensive reforms than others, and the politics of the state plays a major role in determining what is—and what is not—possible. This paper notes the importance of building greater public awareness about the impact and tradeoffs of pension reform. In Democrat-controlled Rhode Island, for example, policymakers began by creating more realistic, and therefore more alarming, estimates of the severity of their state pension system's funding shortfall. They also explained how benefits had evolved to create a much more generous retirement package than had been enjoyed by previous generations of public employees. Ultimately these facts were enough to convince the public that reform was necessary and just, and allow state policymakers to pass and implement much needed changes, in spite of resistance from public-sector unions. In other states, however, such facts have been obscured and sufficient reforms have proved politically impossible, particularly because of the out-sized impact that public sector unions have in state and local elections and political outcomes.

That's why an important part of pension reform should be changing the relationship between politicians and government worker unions.

Consider that in the private sector, when a company manager sits down to negotiate with a union for a compensation package, they have competing interests: The union boss wants higher wages for members, while the manager wants to control employment costs to keep the company profitable. That's not how it works in the public sector. Unions and the politicians often have similar interests: The politician may have promised to raise compensation for government workers as a way of enlisting their support during an election, and the taxpayers—who pay the workers' wages and are liable for their future benefits—lack a robust advocate during such negotiations.

In fact, a key cause of the current pension problems is that promises for increased benefits can be made with few short-term economic costs, although they have tremendous impact on future taxpayers and the state's overall finances.

In Wisconsin, Governor Scott Walker championed legislation that attempted to not only address the state's budget and pension crisis by requiring public workers to contribute more to their future benefits, but also that reformed collective bargaining for some government workers. It capped how much wages could increase in the future (requiring a referendum to approve an increase in excess of inflation), made unionization voluntary, and ceased having governments collect union dues on behalf of the unions. While union leaders vehemently protested, these changes help restore the balance of interests between government workers and the taxpayers who must pay their salaries. As a result of those reforms, the budget situation in Wisconsin has improved dramatically.[14]

FACILITATING PRIVATE SAVINGS

Today, too few Americans are saving for retirement or for a personal financial crisis. A 2013 survey by Bankrate.com found that most Americans (about three-quarters) live paycheck-to-paycheck, meaning that they use all of the money they earn each month for current expenses and save nothing for future needs. While financial planners typically advise that people should have enough savings on hand to cover at least six months of expenses in the event of an emergency, this survey found that just 25 percent of Americans have amassed that cushion. Half of those surveyed had less than three-months worth of expenses, and 27 percent had no savings at all.[15]

There are many reasons that Americans fail to save enough for the future. High joblessness, under-employment, high taxes, and the rising cost of living are among the reasons that more and more American households are finding it difficult just to make ends meet. That's why, most fundamentally, policymakers should be seeking ways to create a positive economic environment—one that is conducive to job creation, rising wages, and more price competition—as a means to improve Americans' financial prospects generally, and make it easier for people to save and behave prudently.

However, policymakers can also attempt to encourage more savings by changing tax laws that discourage savings. Under current law, when Americans purchase a stock or earn interest on an investment, they are taxed on the return generated. That's worth lingering on: Consider that when someone purchases something else, whether it's a new dress or a television, they are not expected to pay a tax every time they use or receive enjoyment from that purchase. Savings alone is singled out for future taxes, even when those investments are made with after-tax dollars.

This double-taxation of savings encourages consumption today and discourages prudent investment in the future. Policymakers should be seeking to reduce, or even eliminate, these taxes in order to change this dynamic and encourage more Americans to save.

Current law does create incentives for savings for specific needs, including retirement and future education costs, by allowing Americans to contribute to accounts tax-free. Allowable contributions to these tax-free accounts are capped each year. Lawmakers ought to consider how to expand such saving options, in order to encourage people to make provisions for other key needs (such as for financial emergency or job loss) and to save a larger portion of what they earn. Such policies could help better position people to weather financial downturns and help boost the economy, by making more capital available for investment.

MyRA—A Flawed Approach to Encouraging Savings

During the 2014 State of the Union address, President Obama announced his intention to launch a new initiative to encourage more Americans to save for retirement. He proposed that the Treasury Department should offer Americans the opportunity to open "My Retirement Accounts," or MyRAs, which would be modeled on the Roth IRA. Under this plan, Americans could open a MyRA with as little as $25 and make contributions of just $5 per month. The accounts would be invested in Treasury bonds, and available only to individuals who earn up to $129,000 per year (or couples up to $191,000). The government would guarantee the accounts against losses, and once any account reaches $15,000, it would have to be rolled over to the private sector into a traditional Roth IRA.

While this sounds like a fine way to encourage Americans to save, as Abby Schacter recently wrote in a policy report for the Independent Women's Forum, MyRAs are an unnecessary government intrusion, which could backfire on Americans' financial security.[16] Encouraging Americans to invest in Treasury bonds would lock them into a very low rate of return, which may be entirely offset by inflation. Setting such a low contribution threshold could send the wrong message, that $5 a month is a sufficient retirement savings plan. The government plan also overlooks that the private banking system already offers similar savings plans, and the government program could encourage some employers to drop their own, better retirement vehicles.

There are better, more effective ways to encourage Americans to save.

CONCLUSION

We want Americans to earn enough money today so that they can save for their retirement and other future needs. That begins with a growing economy that creates jobs and rising wages. Americans also deserve well-conceived public pension programs that are reliable, offer reasonable rates of return, and do not unnecessarily burden taxpayers and the economy.

Policymakers should focus on these goals and make timely changes to government pension systems today so that people can adjust their expectations, start saving more on their own, and prepare for the future. Most importantly, prudent reforms are needed to prevent these programs' current financial challenges from metastasizing into a crisis.

CHAPTER TWELVE

RESTORING AMERICAN CULTURE AND THE FAMILY

BY CHARLOTTE HAYS

Most Americans want the same thing: to live in a civil society where friendly neighborhoods flourish and crime is low.

We intuitively want the satisfaction of supporting ourselves through our own labors. We want children to grow up in nurturing households that prepare them to become worthy adults. We want a society that fosters kindness, civility, and industriousness.

A VISION IN PERIL: THE COARSENING OF SOCIETY

But we know this vision of a flourishing civil society is in jeopardy. We are confronted with this reality whenever we turn on the television, read a newspaper or ride public transportation and hear language that would have shocked previous generations. If you have small children, you are probably concerned that they routinely are exposed to advertisements on television about such formerly intimate topics as how to improve your sex life.

As I write this, MTV's *16 and Pregnant*, a popular reality show that profiles pregnant teens and their "baby daddies," is launching a fifth season. This is not a niche show. When one of the stars went to prison for illegal drugs, the incident rated a segment introduced by George Stephanopoulos on ABC News.

More recently, another reality television star, Kim Kardashian, made the cover of *Vogue*. Kardashian is a household name, of course, who married rapper Kanye West—already the father of her child—in a gazillion-dollar ceremony that merited glittering, wall-to-wall coverage. None of the celebrity journalists who covered it betrayed the slightest discomfort with the—uh—situation. But let's wish her luck—her previous marriage, launched on her reality show, lasted only 72 days.

If modesty and hard work are character traits you value, the Duke University freshman who recently announced that she found it "exciting, thrilling, and empowering" to earn money working as a porn star will concern you. Noting that the coed—who used the nom de porn Belle Knox—had spoken publicly about "rough sex," the liberal *Washington Post* columnist Ruth Marcus penned a column headlined "Hook-Up Culture Run Amok." Marcus wrote:

> Knox's pathetic story wouldn't be worth examining— exploiting?—if it didn't say something deeper about the hook-up culture run amok and the demise of shame. In an age of sexting and Snapchat, of "Girls Gone Wild" and friends with benefits, perhaps it's easy to confuse the relative merits of waitressing and sex work.
>
> "To be perfectly honest, I felt more degraded in a minimum-wage, blue collar, low-paying service job than I ever did doing porn," Knox said of her high school waitressing job.[1]

To be perfectly honest, Belle Knox's story also prompts a frank discussion on the meaning of what used to be called an honest day's work. What accounts for the coarsening of our society—and what can we do to restore civil society?

THE FAMILY: THE TRANSMITTER OF SOCIAL CAPITAL

Many scholars and writers lay the blame for the decline of our civil society squarely upon one phenomenon: the breakdown of the family. Children who do not come from households in which there are two married parents are less likely to acquire the social skills to thrive in society.

As sympathetic as we are to the struggling single mother, she is more likely to raise her kids in poverty. Children from single-parent households are more likely to commit crimes, abuse alcohol and use drugs. It is difficult to get figures on the number of people in prison who grew up in single-parent families. While a Department of Justice profile of jail inmates a dozen years ago found that fifty-six percent were products of a single-parent household or had grown up in the care of a guardian,[2] a more startling 1994 study of juveniles in Wisconsin reported that only 13 percent had grown up in a household with their married parents.[3]

As Manhattan Institute's Kay Hymowitz wrote: "The bottom line is that there is a large body of literature showing that children of single mothers are more likely to commit crimes than children who grow up with their married parents."[4]

A recent *Washington Post* article did some hand-wringing about the disparate number of minority children who were suspended from area schools. The reporter blamed racism. The reporter never considered the likelihood that many of the minority children suspended came from single-parent households, where a put-upon mother was unable to provide the discipline and stability that help children grow up to function well. "The family is the primary transmitter of social capital — the values and character traits that enable people to seize opportunities. Family structure is a primary predictor of an individual's life chances, and family disintegration is the principal cause of the intergenerational transmission of poverty," columnist George Will has written.[5]

THE NEW NORMAL: FORTY PERCENT OF CHILDREN BORN TO UNMARRIED WOMEN

In 1965, when Daniel Patrick Moynihan published *The Moynihan Report,* his sobering study of the African-American family, Moynihan was worried that the illegitimacy rate for African American-children was 23.6 percent. The white illegitimacy rate was 3.07 percent in 1963.

In 2011, the federal government put the illegitimacy rate at 72.3 percent for non-Hispanic blacks and 29.2 percent for non-Hispanic whites. Overall, the illegitimacy rate is 40 percent. One can imagine that Moynihan would be truly alarmed today, as he recognized that the family is the institution that forms our character.

He wrote:

> The role of the family in shaping character and ability is so pervasive as to be easily overlooked. The family is the basic social unit of American life; it is the basic socializing unit. By and large, adult conduct in society is learned as a child. A fundamental insight of psychoanalytic theory, for example, is that the child learns a way of looking at life in his early years through which all later experience is viewed and which profoundly shapes his adult conduct.[6]

"A family is society writ small, where one learns the initial and often the deepest lessons about empathetic behavior," writes the American Enterprise Institute's Nick Schultz in his invaluable and highly readable study *Home Economics: The Consequences of Changing the Family Structure.*[7] Schultz, who focuses on the economic fallout from the breakdown of the family (the word economics comes from the Greek word for family—*oikos)*, reports that children who grow up in single-family households are less likely to have the emotional capability to take the risks associated with entrepreneurship or to have the self-discipline to delay immediate gratification.

Schultz argues that "the collapse of the family is one of the most significant economic facts of our time." Schultz writes that, as the American economy shifts to one that requires more intellectual than physical capital, the decline of the family will be even more significant. But even now he sees a relationship between depressed earnings for low-skilled workers and out of wedlock births.

Schultz recounts attending a dinner in Washington, D.C., with executives from manufacturing companies. The subject was how to create jobs in the manufacturing sector for the poor and middle class. But the talk quickly turned to another topic: jobs that exist but can't be filled because workers aren't prepared. "To be honest," one executive said, "we have a hard time finding people who can simply pass a drug test." In other words, people aren't employable because they don't have the social skills that are associated with growing up in a thriving family.

THE WAR ON THE FAMILY: THE CASUALTIES

We should perhaps not be surprised that the family is not thriving. The feminist movement that became prominent in the 1960s actively attacked the institution of marriage. "I looked through women's studies textbooks and was shocked by how marriage was bashed as a tool of the patriarchy and a trap for women," IWF's Carrie Lukas wrote about researching a book on feminism. She found such attacks as a textbook that included sections on "The Case against Traditional Marriage" and "The Feminine Role in Traditional Marriage: A Setup." This book dismissed what it called the "marriage myth, a mystical tale of love, romance, and marriage" as "utterly false."[8]

But the shifting view of marriage wasn't restricted to feminism. Elsewhere in society other leaders questioned whether the institution was as important as it was believed to be. Steven F. Hayward attended a White House conference on the family during the administration of President Lyndon B. Johnson, held in the wake of the Moynihan Report. Hayward found that the family as an institution was not held in as high esteem as one might have expected:

Soon critics began asking: What's wrong with single-parent families anyway? Andrew Young, whom Martin Luther King tapped as his representative to the White House conference on the issue, said that "there probably isn't anything wrong with the Negro family as it exists." The concern with family stability, critics said in a now-familiar refrain, was an attempt to "impose middle class values" on the poor. In fact, it was asserted, the black female headed household is a "cultural pattern superior in its vitality to middle-class mores."[9]

Predictably, such attitudes have harmed no segment of society more than the poor. The more affluent experimented with rejecting marriage, but have rediscovered it as the best way to rear successful children. This has created what the Manhattan Institute's Hymowitz dubbed "the marriage gap:" educated women marry before having children, while low income women are more likely to go it alone. "Why would women working for a pittance at supermarket cash registers decide to have children without getting married while women writing briefs at Debevoise & Plimpton, who could easily afford to go it alone, insist on finding husbands before they start families?" Hymowitz asked in her 2006 book, *Marriage and Caste in America: Separate and Unequal Families in a Post-Marital Age*. One of the reasons is that marriage is now less likely to be held out as the norm, and indeed low-income young men have lost what Hymowitz calls "the life script" for rearing children and assuming adult responsibilities that benefit both their children and their own personal prospects.[10]

As usual, it is those who can least afford it who pay the price for society's newly cool attitude towards marriage. While educated women are rearing their children in two-parent households, worrying more about an Ivy League education than survival, the women who are struggling to rear children in single-parent households, more likely than not in crime-ridden neighborhoods, are casualties of the war on marriage.

THE WAR ON WORK

The American Enterprise Institute's Charles Murray—who, like Hymowitz is a pioneer in exploring the causes and effects of the marriage gap— writes about the decline of the "founding virtues" in his 2012 book *Coming Apart.* One of these founding virtues is industriousness, a virtue in Western society since Hesiod, the Greek poet, celebrated it in "Works and Days," one of the earliest poems in the western canon.

The Founders, according to Murray, shared "a bone-deep American assumption that life is to be spent in getting ahead through hard work, making a better life for oneself and one's children." The work ethic has been so strong in our history that Murray wrote, "If just one American virtue may be said to be defining, industriousness is probably it."[11]

But Murray and others have found a decline in the industriousness of Americans. The clearest way to see it is through workforce participation numbers. Ninety-two million Americans are not in the work force—they don't have jobs and they aren't looking for jobs. Many of these people undoubtedly searched for jobs and have given up in despair.

However, what Murray calls the "stigma against idleness" has softened. Social Security disability claims are at an all-time high. Congress broadened requirements for disability insurance, and there is a whole legal industry aimed at helping people obtain it. "As a result, many able-bodied Americans have been granted government paychecks for life, crowding out our ability to direct needed resources to the genuinely infirm," Avik Roy wrote at the *Forbes* magazine blog.[12] We are currently paying about $200 billion a year for the disability program. This situation is not merely economically unsustainable. It is spiritually unsustainable: work gives meaning and purpose to our lives.

TAKE A STAND FOR LOW-INCOME KIDS WHO DESERVE A TWO-PARENT FAMILY

As both Kay Hymowitz and Charles Murray have pointed out, more affluent families recognize the value of having two parents involved in the project of child rearing. But in their condescension and fear of not appearing broad-minded, they won't take a stand for low-income kids who deserve the same advantage.

Murray has written:

> The best thing that the new upper class can do to provide that reinforcement [of values needed to succeed] is to drop its condescending "nonjudgmentalism." Married, educated people who work hard and conscientiously raise their kids shouldn't hesitate to voice their disapproval of those who defy these norms. When it comes to marriage and the work ethic, the new upper class must start preaching what it practices.[13]

Nobody likes a scold, and scolding doesn't accomplish much anyway. That is now what we advocate. But being clear about the importance of the two-parent family is the beginning of the restoration of our culture. A child is more likely to acquire the discipline and other values needed to thrive in a household with her married parents. It should be noted that, according to a variety of studies, cohabitating, unmarried parents are a poor substitute for a household with two married, biological parents.[14]

W. Bradford Wilcox, head of the National Marriage Project at the University of Virginia, said that half of the births to high-school educated mothers are out of wedlock and that the very notion of marriage is fading among the least educated segment of our population. Unless society has the courage to take a stand for marriage, and not just for the affluent, more people will lose what Hymowitz calls the "life script."

If we as a society seek to elevate the poor instead of tearing down the successful, we must put more emphasis on marriage. We do not seek to denigrate single-mothers, who have special burdens in the project of childrearing, but we must be very clear that single-parent households do not, as a rule, do the best by the children.

ELIMINATE BARRIERS TO FAMILY FORMATION

Well-intended Great Society programs beginning in the 1960s ended up having a destructive effect on the family. It is time to reverse this trend by promoting marriage instead of entitlements. But can government do anything to promote marriage?

Individuals and associations are better at creating social capital than government. But government can get out of the way by eliminating programs that harm families by fostering intergenerational poverty, a topic that is discussed in more detail in chapter ten.

There is no shortage of conservative thought on how to accomplish this goal. In an important article in *Commentary* magazine, for example, Arthur Brooks, president of the American Enterprise Institute, suggested what he called a "social justice agenda" for conservatives who have largely ceded the term social justice to their opponents. The headline was "Be Open Handed toward Your Brothers," and it acknowledged a place for a safety net—but it cautioned against allowing the safety net to become a permanent way of life.[15]

Some conservatives advocate increasing the Earned Income Tax Credit, an idea worthy of discussion. It is essential to eliminate the marriage penalty in our tax system, and, for families that have been able to accumulate resources by virtue of their own exertions, we should eliminate the death tax and allow them to pass the fruit of their labors on to the next generation rather than to the government.

THE RESTORATION OF WORK

A CBS News headline captured a grim reality: "Millions of Americans Forced to Work Part Time."[16] The Department of Labor reported in the spring of 2014 that 7.4 million Americans were forced into part-time jobs, but would have preferred full-time positions. There is good reason that these people aspire to full-time jobs: The simple truth is a middle-class life is unsustainable on a part-time job. A full-time job is the key to making it into and remaining in the middle class.

Jobs and opportunities have been plentiful during most of the American past, creating unprecedented upward mobility. If one had to distill the essence of the American dream into two words, those words might be "upward mobility." While that was our past, government regulations and programs today depress jobs.

The Patient Protection and Affordable Care Act makes it illegal for any business, regardless of the precariousness of the enterprise, that employs 50 or more full-time workers not to provide health insurance. Instead of ensuring that more people get health insurance the law appears to be ensuring that fewer people get full-time work. But it is not the only piece of legislation that has stymied job creation. We now have so many regulations that the United States is becoming a less attractive place for entrepreneurs. We need to get rid of many of the laws that get rid of jobs.

We also need to recapture our belief in the value of work. A legislator recently praised the Affordable Care Act because it makes it easier for somebody to leave a job without the next job lined up or to become a poet. Not many people have the ability to be professional poets, and it is good discipline, not to mention a way to pay the bills, to remain employed, even if the job doesn't come with the title CEO or Poet Laureate. We must, as our predecessors did, come to recognize again that honest work is a way to give our lives meaning. We must recognize government dependence, whether for low-income or middle-class or even affluent people, for the entangling and debilitating thing that it is.

CIVIL AND RELIGIOUS INSTITUTIONS

When Alexis de Tocqueville visited the United States in the early nineteenth century, he was impressed with the variety of civic and neighborhood associations that formed the civic life of the nation, many of them deriving from religious convictions. "I met with several kinds of associations in America of which I confess I had no previous notion; and I have often admired the extreme skill with which the inhabitants of the United States succeed in proposing a common object for the exertions of a great many men and in inducing them voluntarily to pursue it," de Tocqueville wrote.

Unfortunately, the government has begun the process of replacing many of these voluntary organizations in the civic sphere. Religious liberty is under attack, and religion is often the force that has inspired voluntary charitable or civic action. Perhaps the most notable example is the Little Sisters of the Poor, an order of Catholic nuns who devote themselves to the care of the indigent elderly, who would be required by the government to violate their religious faith by paying for insurance coverage for contraception. If they refuse, they face enormous fines. The future of the nuns' work is unclear.

To once again become a flourishing and vibrant society, we must see government shrink and the associations of the kind de Tocqueville so admired expand to fill the void and make the United States once again a nation of neighborliness and kindness.

WOMEN AND MEN—OR LADIES AND GENTLEMEN

When the Costa Concordia, a luxury cruise ship, sank off the coast of Tuscany in 2012, male passengers and crew members pushed their way past grandmothers and pregnant women to save themselves. The contrast with the Titanic a century earlier, when men sacrificed their lives for women, was inevitable. We are not advocating that women must behave and be treated like medieval queens or Victorian ladies. We believe that women can have fulfilling lives commanding from the corner office. But we also believe that the restoration of gracious behavior between the sexes would have a profound effect on turning the tide to a more livable society. It could begin with recognition that the hook-up culture on college campuses is harmful to girls—and, yes, to young men, who also suffer from casual, intimate encounters that call for no responsibility on their part.

We have talked a great deal about policy in this little book, but for society to flourish, policy can't accomplish anything unless we have the culture to give the foundation. Perhaps we should close with the words of a Founder. Recognizing the centrality of culture, Thomas Jefferson wrote, "It is the manners and spirit of a people which preserve a republic in vigour. A degeneracy in these is a canker which soon eats to the heart of its laws and constitution."[17]

WHAT YOU CAN DO TO BUILD A STRONGER AMERICA

BY CARRIE LUKAS AND SABRINA SCHAEFFER

ontrary to what many progressives today would have you believe, government alone doesn't create change. Individuals and communities shape the world we live in.

Today's more modern, flexible workplace didn't emerge from a set of government laws; it's the result of new technology, evolving gender roles, and demands from both men and women to have more balance in their lives. Progressives want a small group of government elites to institute top-down changes that they think are best for everyone, but we know that it's best to have individuals refashion society so that we have a true diversity of options and thriving communities that respond to the needs and preferences of the people within them.

This book has presented that vision of America. It's a portrait of what the country could look like if we restore government to its proper place, and return power to the people so they can create a stronger civil society. This America would have a vibrant economy and a thriving business arena, creating a diversity of job opportunities; a patient-centered health system;

a growing and competitive energy sector; a strong, targeted safety net and a dynamic education system. It's possible to steer our country back to having a healthier culture, where individuals, not the government, serve as the chief executive, and where hard work pays off.

While government isn't the sole source of change and advancement, our laws do shape the world we live in. High taxes, soaring deficits, and onerous regulations strangle job creation, leaving all of us poorer and less free. Ill-conceived health care laws and education systems mean fewer choices and a less bright future. Safety-net programs meant to help can become a community's worst enemy if they undermine the foundation of a healthy culture and discourage productive behavior.

Ultimately realizing the vision of a stronger America isn't just the work of legislators and politicians. We can all contribute to this process and build a better society. Here's a few ways that you can help.

TALK ABOUT THESE ISSUES AND BUILD SUPPORT FOR REAL REFORM

Americans are frustrated with the direction of our country and communities, but they are also often frustrated with the political process. When politicians offer "change" every two or four years, and nothing ever seems to change for the better, it's easy to be discouraged.

But we can't give up. We need to get involved and encourage people to not just rally around campaign slogans, but to build a real understanding of and support for positive policy reforms that move our country in the right direction.

Increasingly, people don't trust the media anymore than they trust politicians—and for good reason. Instead of relying on such sources, people now tend to get their political and policy ideas from their friends and family members. That means you have a vital role to play in becoming a thought-leader among your friends. Get up to speed on the major policy issues of the day and start talking to people about what you know and believe.

You can hold informal meetings with your friends and family, like a book club but featuring issues and policy topics. You could build those meetings into a grassroots chapter of the Independent Women's Network. You could share more information with your social media network and make your opinions known by writing and submitting articles to your state and local newspapers. As was described earlier in this book, technology has truly democratized the information-sharing and political process. That means your voice can be heard and you can have a major impact.

GET INVOLVED IN THE LIVES OF THOSE AROUND YOU

We want public policies that encourage productive behavior and create opportunity for Americans everywhere. But a society in which government is not a dominant force must have a strong civic society to fill that void. Women, in particular, have a long history in America of helping advance limited government values, fostering a relationship between citizen and state in which individuals are sovereign over government, and playing an active role in their communities.

If you know someone who is out of work, see how you can help her in the job search process. Review her applications and make introductions. Encourage her to look outside her field and current living area and take a chance on something new. Talk about the opportunities to gain new skills online.

Friends and families frustrated by their current job situation may also benefit from hearing more about the tradeoffs we all face when selecting jobs, and they should be encouraged to think of ways that they can improve their situations. And we want to encourage women in particular to consider their choices carefully in order to maximize their success, but also their happiness. Similarly, younger Americans may need to hear more about the importance of family formation in building lasting success.

Our lawmakers have work to do in creating a policy environment that creates more economic growth; but ultimately we are all responsible for our own success or failure. So do your part to help those around you make the most of the opportunities they have.

SUPPORT THE LOCAL, COMMUNITY BASED ORGANIZATIONS THAT ARE HELPING YOUR NEIGHBORHOOD

As you read in this book, a government safety net and transfer programs can create as many problems as they solve. We've learned that not only does this government assistance actually encourage many individuals to abdicate their responsibilities, but also it's destroying much of our civil society. Too much government simply crowds out the churches, synagogues, schools, and neighborhoods that are best equipped to actually help those in their communities who are in need. That's why it's so important to support the local organizations that are doing important work to help those in need in your community.

We all know that there are many people who fall on hard times and need assistance to rebuild their lives. That takes more than money—though resources are often also needed—it also takes caring individuals who are willing to work with people, treat them with respect as individuals with potential, and help them identify steps they can take to move toward a path of independence and greater fulfillment.

There are organizations throughout the country that are making an important difference so that Americans are not "Bowling Alone"— mentoring kids, feeding the hungry, helping those seeking jobs with interview skills, supporting those leaving the prison system to transition back into society, caring for veterans in need, and the list could go on and on. Each and every one of us has something to add to one of these efforts, whether that's with your time or your money. Choose wisely so that your investment makes a real impact, but keep in mind that it's up to all of us to help fill these important roles in our communities.

And even closer to us than the safety net of charitable community organizations is the safety net of family. If you are a loving and supportive family member then you are already doing some of the most important work to knit together the moral fabric of our country. Strong family households contribute to a thriving economy, but they are also the starting point for the next generation to learn how to treat others well, embrace a work ethic, and live upstanding lives.

IMPROVE YOUR OWN LIFE

Of course, your first job should be to assess how you are doing personally, and if you are embracing the change you hope to see around you. Take a look at how you have been building your career and your relationships. How can you do better? What are your dreams for the future? What steps do you need to take to get there?

We all have areas in which we can improve, so it helps to take a good look at where you are and where you hope to be next year, and the year after that. There is no time like the present, so dedicate yourself to making the most of your talents and opportunities today.

FINAL THOUGHTS

America does not have to be a nation on the brink of disaster. And women don't need to be living on the brink of economic despair.

America—which has always been the Land of Opportunity—can once again become a nation on the brink of unprecedented economic growth, greater security and personal fulfillment. Realizing that vision will take hard work from all of us to improve our local communities as well as our national policies. It will require us resisting more of the same top-down policies. And it means that we have to use our voices to tell those around us about the benefits of limited government and greater freedom.

We are already working hard to advance this vision.

Will you join us?

We hope you will.

ENDNOTES

CHAPTER ONE
1   The author is grateful to Jared Meyer and Jason Russell of the Manhattan Institute for research assistance. All errors are her own.
2   "Gross Domestic Product: First Quarter 2014 (Third Estimate), Bureau of Economic Analysis, U.S. Department of Commerce, June 25, 2014. Available at: http://www.bea.gov/newsreleases/national/gdp/2014/pdf/gdp1q14_3rd.pdf
3   Bureau of Labor Statistics, "Current Employment Statistics," July 2014.
4   "Table A-15. Alternative measures of labor underutilization," Economic News Release, Bureau of Labor Statistics, July 3, 2014. Available at: http://www.bls.gov/news.release/empsit.t15.htm.
5   "The Employment Situation—June 2014," Bureau of Labor Statistics, July 3, 2014. Available at: http://www.bls.gov/news.release/pdf/empsit.pdf.
6   *Ibid.*
7   Bureau of Labor Statistics, "Job Openings and Labor Turnover Survey," March 2014.
8   Bureau of Economic Analysis, "International Economic Accounts," January 2014.
9   Lawrence J. Lau in discussion with the author, 2013.
10 National Taxpayer Advocate, "Fiscal Year 2014 Objectives Report to Congress," June 2013.
11 Markle, Kevin S. and Douglas A. Shackelford, "The Impact of Headquarter and Subsidiary Locations on Multinationals' Effective Tax Rates," working paper National Bureau of Economic Research, 2013.
12 Levin, Carl, "Offshore Profit Shifting and the U.S. Tax Code," Senate Permanent Subcommittee on Investigations, September 2012.
13 International Energy Agency, "World Energy Outlook 2012," November 2012.
14 Mills, Mark P., "Where the Jobs Are: Small Businesses Unleash America's Energy Employment Boom," Manhattan Institute, February 2014.

15 Slaughter, Matthew J., "How America Loses a Job Every 43 Seconds," *Wall Street Journal*, March 25, 2014.
16 Reich, Michael and Ken Jacobs, "All Economics Is Local," *New York Times*, March 22, 2014.
17 Kasprak, Nicholas A., "State to State Migration Data," Tax Foundation, 2013.
18 Neumark, David, J.M. Ian Salas, and William Wascher, "Revisiting the Minimum Wage-Employment Debate: Throwing Out the Baby with the Bathwater?," forthcoming in *Industrial and Labor Relations Review.*
19 Congressional Budget Office, "The Effects of a Minimum-Wage Increase on Employment and Family Income," February 2014.
20 "A Statement to Federal Policy Makers," March 2014.
21 Mulligan, Casey B., *The Redistribution Recession: How Labor Market Distortions Contracted the Economy*, New York: Oxford University Press, November 2012.

CHAPTER TWO
1 Marketing Charts Staff, "Women in Mature Economies Control Household Spending," *Marketing Charts*, May 18, 2010. Available at: http://www.marketingcharts.com/wp/traditional/women-in-mature-economies-control-household-spending-12931/.
2 Romina Boccia and Matthew Sabas, "Booze, Pole Dancing, and Luxurious Hotels: Top 10 Examples of Government Waste in 2013," The Heritage Foundation, *The Foundry,* December 30, 2013. Available at: http://blog.heritage.org/2013/12/30/mb-1230-booze-pole-dancing-luxurious-hotels-top-10-examples-government-waste-2013/.
3 Charles Blahous, "Why We Have Federal Deficits," Mercatus Center, *Expert Commentary*, November 14, 2013. Available at: http://mercatus.org/expert_commentary/why-we-have-federal-deficits.
4 Matthew Spalding, "America's Founders and the Principles of Foreign Policy: Sovereign Independence, National Interests, and the Cause of Liberty in the World," The Heritage Foundation, *First Principles Series Report* No. 33, October 15, 2010. Available at: http://www.heritage.org/research/reports/2010/10/americas-founders-and-the-principles-of-foreign-policy-sovereign-independence.
5 Romina Boccia, "The Federal Budget in Pictures, 2014." Available at: http://www.heritage.org/federalbudget/where-tax-dollar-will-go. Based on data by the Congressional Budget Office, The 2013 Long-Term Budget Outlook, September 17, 2013. Available at: http://www.cbo.gov/publication/44521.
6 Romina Boccia, Alison Acosta Fraser, and Emily Goff, "Federal Spending by the Numbers, 2013: Government Spending Trends in Graphics, Tables, and Key Points," The Heritage Foundation, *Special Report* No. 140, August 20, 2013. Available at: http://www.heritage.org/research/reports/2013/08/federal-spending-by-the-numbers-2013.
7 Katrina Trinko, "Heritage Experts Weigh In On Massive Omnibus Spending Bill," The Heritage Foundation, *The Foundry*, January 13, 2014. Available at: http://blog.heritage.org/2014/01/13/heritage-experts-weigh-massive-omnibus-spending-bill/.
8 Romina Boccia, Michael Sargent, and John Fleming, "2014 Federal Budget in Pictures," The Heritage Foundation, 2014. Available at: http://www.heritage.org/federalbudget/.
9 Romina Boccia, "How to Make Social Security Work Better for Women," The Heritage Foundation *The Foundry,* October 26, 2012. Available at: http://blog.heritage.org/2012/10/26/obamas-economic-patriotism-is-failing-women-in-retirement/.
10 "Federal Tax Revenue by Source, 1934 – 2018," Tax Foundation, November 21, 2013. Available at: http://taxfoundation.org/article/federal-tax-revenue-source-1934-2018.

11   Veronique de Rugy, "Progressivity of Taxes in OECD Countries, Mid-2000s," Mercatus Center, January 3, 2012. Available at: http://mercatus.org/ publication/progressivity-taxes-oecd-countries-mid-2000s.

12   "Federal Tax Revenue by Source, 1934 – 2018," Tax Foundation, November 21, 2013. Available at: http://taxfoundation.org/article/federal-tax-revenue-source-1934-2018.

13   Laurence J. Kotlikoff, "Abolish the Corporate Income Tax," *The New York Times,* January 5, 2014. Available at: http://www.nytimes.com/2014/01/06/ opinion/abolish-the-corporate-income-tax.html?_r=0.

14   Roberton Williams, "The Numbers: What are the federal government's sources of revenue?" Tax Policy Center *The Tax Policy Briefing Book*, September 13, 2011. Available at: http://www.taxpolicycenter.org/briefing-book/background/numbers/revenue.cfm.

15   National Taxpayer Advocate, "Time for Tax Reform is Now," *Annual Report to Congress*, 2014. Available at: http://www.taxpayeradvocate.irs.gov/2012-Annual-Report/tax-code-complexity/.

16   Marsida Harremi, "The Flat Tax and Efficiency of Fiscal System," *Academic Journal of Interdisciplinary Studies*, Vol 2, No 8, October 2013. Available at: http://www.mcser.org/journal/index.php/ajis/article/viewFile/756/787.

17   Curtis Dubay, "Tax Extenders an Opportunity to Improve the Tax Code," The Heritage Foundation, Issue Brief No. 4187, March 31, 2014, http://www. heritage.org/research/reports/2014/03/tax-extenders-an-opportunity-to-improve-the-tax-code.

18   Romina Boccia and Matthew Sabas, "Booze, Pole Dancing, and Luxurious Hotels: Top 10 Examples of Government Waste in 2013," The Heritage Foundation *The Foundry,* December 30, 2013. Available at: http://blog. heritage.org/2013/12/30/mb-1230-booze-pole-dancing-luxurious-hotels-top-10-examples-government-waste-2013/.

19   U.S. Government Accountability Office, *Actions Needed to Reduce Fragmentation, Overlap, and Duplication and Achieve Other Financial Benefits,* April 9, 2013. Available at: http://www.gao.gov/products/gao-13-279sp.

20   Jerry Brito, "The Brac Commission as a Model for Federal Spending Reform," *The Georgetown Journal of Law & Public Policy,* Vol. 9, No. 1 (Winter 2011), pp. 132-156. Available at: http://jerrybrito.com/pdf/Brito-BRAC.pdf.

21   David M. Primo, "The Uses and Misuses of Budget Data," Mercatus Center, March 11, 2014. Available at: http://mercatus.org/sites/default/files/Primo_ UsesandMisuses_v1.pdf.

22   Salim Furth, "Debt is a real drag in any season," *The Washington Times*, February 27, 2013, http://www.washingtontimes.com/news/2013/feb/27/ furth-debt-is-a-real-drag-in-any-season/.

23   F. F. Wiley, "Revisiting the Reinhart-Rogoff Kerfuffle, Part 2," *Cyniconomics,* February 20, 2014, http://www.cyniconomics.com/2014/02/20/revisiting-reinhart-rogoff-and-govt-debt-part-2/.

24   Veronique de Rugy and Jason J. Fichtner, "Improper Federal Payments Waste over $100 billion in 2012," Mercatus Center, February 17, 2014. Available at: http://mercatus.org/publication/improper-federal-payments-waste-over-100-billion-2012.

CHAPTER 3

1   "U.S. Ranks Just 42nd in Life Expectancy," *Associated Press*, August 11, 2007. Available at: http://www.nbcnews.com/id/20228552/ns/health-health_ care/t/us-ranks-just-nd-life-expectancy/#.U2BXleZdWHd.

2   "The World Fact Book," Central Intelligence Agency, 2009. Available at: https://www.cia.gov/library/publications/the-world-factbook/ rankorder/2091rank.html .

3   Robert L. Ohsfeldt and John E. Schneider, *The Business of Health*, American Enterprise Institute Press, September 1, 2006. Available at: http://www.aei. org/book/health/health care-reform/the-business-of-health/.

4   Olshansky SJ, Passaro DJ, Hershow RC, Layden J, Carnes BA, Brody J, Hayflick L, Butler RN, Allison DB, and Ludwig DS, "A Potential Decline in Life Expectancy in the United States in the 21st Century," *New England Journal of Medicine*, 352:11, pp. 1138-1145. Available at: http://www.ncbi.nlm.nih.gov/pubmed/15784668.

5   H.E. Frech, Stephen T. Parente, and John Hoff, "U.S. Health Care: A Reality Check on Cross-Country Comparisons," American Enterprise Institute, July 11, 2012. Available at: http://www.aei.org/outlook/health/global-health/us-health-care-a-reality-check-on-cross-country-comparisons/.

6   June E. O'Neill and Dave M. O'Neill, "Health Status, Health Care and Inequality: Canada vs. the U.S.," National Bureau of Economic Research, September 2007. Available at: http://www.nber.org/papers/w13429.pdf.

7   *The World Health Report*, World Health Organization, 2000. Available at: http://www.who.int/whr/2000/en/annex01_en.pdf.

8   June E. O'Neill and Dave M. O'Neill, "Health Status, Health Care and Inequality: Canada vs. the U.S.," National Bureau of Economic Research, September 2007. Available at: http://www.nber.org/papers/w13429.pdf.

9   Michel P. Coleman et al, "Cancer Survival in Five Continents: A Worldwide Population-Based Study," *The Lancet Oncology*, Volume 9, Issue 8, August 2008, pp 730–756. Available at: http://www.thelancet.com/journals/lanonc/article/PIIS1470204508701797/abstract.

10   Glen Whitman and Raymond Raad, "Bending the Productivity Curve," Cato Institute, September 18, 2009. Available at: http://www.cato.org/sites/cato.org/files/pubs/pdf/pa654.pdf.

11   *Ibid.*

12   Robert Helms, "Tax Policy and the History of the Health Insurance Industry," American Enterprise Institute, February 29, 2008, pp 6-7. Available at: http://www.taxpolicycenter.org/tpccontent/healthconference_helms.pdf.

13   "History of Health Insurance Benefits," Employee Benefit Research Institute, March 2002. Available at: http://www.ebri.org/publications/facts/index.cfm?fa=0302fact.

14   Stephen F. Gohmann and Myra J. McCrickard, "The Effect of State Mandates on Health Insurance Premiums," *The Journal of Private Enterprise*, 2009. Available at: http://journal.apee.org/images/e/ee/Spring2009_5.pdf.

15   "Total Number of Medicare Beneficiaries," Kaiser Family Foundation. Available at: http://kff.org/medicare/state-indicator/total-medicare-beneficiaries/.

16   C. Eugene Steuerle and Stephanie Rennane, "How Lifetime Benefits and Contributions Point the Way Toward Reforming Our Senior Entitlement Programs," Urban Institute, August 2011. Available at: http://www.urban.org/uploadedpdf/1001553-Reforming-Our-Senior-Entitlement-Programs.pdf.

17   "Totally Medicaid Enrollment, FY 2010," Kaiser Family Foundation. Available at: http://kff.org/medicaid/state-indicator/total-medicaid-enrollment/.

18   "Policy Basics: Where Do Our State Tax Dollars Go?" Center for Budget and Policy Priorities, March 27, 2014. Available at: http://www.cbpp.org/cms/?fa=view&id=2783.

19   Robert E. Moffit, "Obamacare: Impact on Doctors," Heritage Foundation WebMemo No. 2895, May 11, 2010. Available at: http://www.heritage.org/research/reports/2010/05/obamacare-impact-on-doctors.

20   "Estimates for the Insurance Coverage Provisions of the Affordable Care Act Updated for the Recent Supreme Court Decision," Congressional Budget

Office, Table 3 (year 2012), July 2012. Available at: http://cbo.gov/sites/default/files/cbofiles/attachments/43472-07-24-2012-CoverageEstimates.pdf.

21 Explaining Health Care Reform: Questions about Health Insurance Subsidies," Kaiser Family Foundation, 7/2012. Available at: http://kaiserfamilyfoundation.files.wordpress.com/2013/01/7962-02.pdf.

22 Kurt Glesa and Chris Carlson, "Age Band Compression Under Health Care Reform," *Contingencies*, 2013. Available at: http://www.nahu.org/meetings/capitol/2013/attendees/jumpdrive/contingencies20130102_1357146485000 c7cc7dd5e1_pp.pdf.

23 "Employer-sponsored Coverage Background and FAQs for the Health Insurance Marketplace," Centers for Medicare and Medicaid Services. Available at: http://marketplace.cms.gov/getofficialresources/training-materials/background-and-faqs-on-employer-sponsored-coverage.pdf.

24 Kurt Glesa and Chris Carlson, "Age Band Compression Under Health Care Reform," *Contingencies*, 2013. Available at: http://www.nahu.org/meetings/capitol/2013/attendees/jumpdrive/contingencies20130102_1357146485000 c7cc7dd5e1_pp.pdf.

25 Larry Levitt and Gary Claxton, "What is a Mini-Med Plan?" Kaiser Family Foundation, July 5, 2011. Available at: http://kff.org/health-reform/perspective/what-is-a-mini-med-plan/.

26 Grace-Marie Turner, "It's Fact, Not Anecdote, That ObamaCare is Turning Us Into a Part-Time Nation," *Forbes*, August 27, 2013. Available at: http://www.forbes.com/sites/gracemarieturner/2013/08/27/its-fact-not-anecdote-that-obamacare-is-turning-us-into-a-part-time-nation/.

27 "Medicaid Expansion," American Public Health Association. Available at: http://www.apha.org/advocacy/Health+Reform/ACAbasics/medicaid.htm.

28 *National Federation of Independent Businesses v. Sebelius*, Supreme Court of the United States, June 28, 2012. Available at: http://www2.bloomberglaw.com/public/desktop/document/Natl_Federation_of_Independent_Business_v_Sebelius_No_Nos_11393_1.

29 "Status of State Action on the Medicaid Expansion Decision, 2014," Kaiser Family Foundation. Available at: http://kff.org/health-reform/state-indicator/state-activity-around-expanding-medicaid-under-the-affordable-care-act/.

30 "Policy Basics: Where Do Our State Tax Dollars Go?," Center for Budget and Policy Priorities, March 27, 2014. Available at: http://www.cbpp.org/cms/?fa=view&id=2783,

31 "Medicaid Expansion," American Public Health Association. Available at: http://www.apha.org/advocacy/Health+Reform/ACAbasics/medicaid.htm.

32 Lindsay Holst, "President Obama: 8 Million People Have Signed Up for Prive Health Coverage," The White House Blog, April 17, 2014. Available at: http://www.whitehouse.gov/blog/2014/04/17/president-obama-8-million-people-have-signed-private-health-coverage.

33 Ronald Reagan, "Remarks at Governor's Conference on Medicaid," San Francisco, 1968. Available at: http://theccwr.org/reagan-template.html.

34 Robert E. Moffit, "Obamacare: Impact on Doctors," Heritage Foundation WebMemo No. 2895, May 11, 2010. Available at: http://www.heritage.org/research/reports/2010/05/obamacare-impact-on-doctors.

35 Sandra L. Decker, "In 2011 Nearly One-Third of Physicians Said They Would Not Accept New Medicaid Patients, But Rising Fees May Help," *Health Affairs*, 2011. Available at: http://content.healthaffairs.org/content/31/8/1673.abstract.

36   Avik Roy, "The Medicaid Mess: How ObamaCare Makes It Worse," The Manhattan Institute, March 2012. Available at: http://www.manhattan-institute.org/pdf/ir_8.pdf.

37   Hadley Heath Manning, "The Independent Payment Advisory Board," Independent Women's Forum, July 2011. Available at: http://www.iwf.org/files/c7e6569c3661053a248ab866e97ee597.pdf.

38   Sarah Palin, "Statement on Current Health Care Debate," Facebook post, 8/7/2009. Available at: https://www.facebook.com/note.php?note_id=113851103434.

39   Avik Roy, "Are Paul Ryan's Medicare Spending Targets Impossible?" Forbes, April 9, 2011. Available at: http://www.forbes.com/sites/aroy/2011/04/09/obamacares-medicare-cuts-are-as-deep-as-ryancares/.

40   Kaiser Family Foundation Health Tracking Poll, Figure 12, 3/2013. Available at: http://kff.org/health-reform/poll-finding/march-2013-tracking-poll/.

41   National Federation of Independent Businesses v. Sebelius, Supreme Court of the United States, June 28, 2012. Available at: http://www2.bloomberglaw.com/public/desktop/document/Natl_Federation_of_Independent_Business_v_Sebelius_No_Nos_11393_1.

42   "Essential Health Benefits," Department of Health and Human Services. Available at: https://www.health care.gov/glossary/essential-health-benefits/.

43   "Policy Notifications and Current Status, by State," Associated Press, December 26, 2013. Available at: http://news.yahoo.com/policy-notifications-current-status-state-204701399.html.

44   Avik Roy, "The Biggest Beneficiary of the Contraception Mandate? Drug Companies," The Atlantic, March 6, 2012. Available at: http://www.theatlantic.com/business/archive/2012/03/the-biggest-beneficiary-of-the-contraception-mandate-drug-companies/254048/.

45   "HHS Information Central," The Becket Fund. Available at: http://www.becketfund.org/hhsinformationcentral/.

46   Chris Conover, "Seriously? The Republicans Have No Health Plan?" Forbes, August 28, 2013. Available at: http://www.forbes.com/sites/theapothecary/2013/08/28/seriously-the-republicans-have-no-health-plan/.

47   "OECD Health Statistics 2013," Organization for Economic Cooperation and Development. Available at: http://www.oecd.org/els/health-systems/oecdhealthdata2013-frequentlyrequesteddata.htm.

48   "National Health Expenditure Projections 2011-2021," Centeres for Medicare and Medicaid Services. Available at: http://www.cms.gov/Research-Statistics-Data-and-Systems/Statistics-Trends-and-Reports/NationalHealthExpendData/Downloads/Proj2011PDF.pdf.

49   Grace-Marie Turner and Tyler Hartsfield, "Twenty-Seven ObamaCare Changes," National Review, November 15, 2013. Available at: http://www.nationalreview.com/article/364080/twenty-seven-obamacare-changes-grace-marie-turner-tyler-hartsfield.

50   Tarren Bragdon, "Florida's Medicaid Reform Shows the Way to Improve Health, Increase Satisfaction, and Control Costs," The Heritage Foundation, November 9, 2011. Available at: http://www.medicaidcure.org/wp-content/uploads/2012/09/Medicaid-Cure-Floridas-Medicaid-Reform-Pilot.pdf.

51   "Medicare," U.S. Congressman Paul Ryan Website. Available at: http://paulryan.house.gov/issues/issue/?IssueID=9969#.U2eeIq1dWHc.

52   Paul Howard and Yevgeniy Feyman, "A Decade of Success: How Competition Drives Savings in Medicare Part D," Manhattan Institute, December 16, 2013. Available at: http://www.manhattan-institute.org/html/mpr_16.htm#.U2W5na1dWHc.

CHAPTER 4

1   Kim Parker and Wendy Wang, "Modern Parenthood: Roles of Moms and Dads Converge as They Balance Work and Family," Pew Research Social & Demographic Trends, March 14, 2013, p. 5. Available at: http://www.pewsocialtrends.org/files/2013/03/FINAL_modern_parenthood_03-2013.pdf.

2   Katty Kay and Claire Shipman, *Womenomics: Write Your Own Rules for Success*, Harper Collins, 2009, p. xix.

3   Matthew Wiswall and Basit Zafar, "Determinants of College Major Choice: Identification Using an Information Experiment," Federal Reserve Bank of New York, Staff Report No. 500, June 2011, Revised January 2013.

4   Mika Brezinski with Daniel Paisner, *All Things At Once*, Weinstein Books, 2009.

5   "Women in the Labor Force: A Databook," Bureau of Labor Statistics, BLS Reports February 2013,. Available at: http://www.bls.gov/cps/wlf-databook-2012.pdf.

6   U.S. Department of Education, National Center for Education Statistics, *The Condition of Education in 2012*, NCES 2012-045, 2012, Indicator 47. Available at: http://nces.ed.gov/pubsearch/pubsinfo.asp?pubid=2012045. And, Diana Furchgott-Roth, *Women's Figures: An Illustrated Guide to the Economic Progress of Women in America,* 2012 Edition, pp 41-45. And Nathan Bell, Council of Graduate Schools. Available at: http://www.cgsnet.org/2010-press-coverage.

7   Furchgott-Roth, *Women's Figures*, 12.

8   "The Bottom Line: Connecting Corporate Performance and Gender Diversity," Catalyst, January 2004, p.3.

9   Ekaterina Walter, "The Top 30 Stats You Need to Know When Marketing to Women," thenextweb, January 24, 2012. Available at: http://thenextweb.com/socialmedia/2012/01/24/the-top-30-stats-you-need-to-know-when-marketing-to-women/#!u56L6.

10 Stuart Feil, "Bread Buyer and Breadwinner: As Women's Roles Shift, So Does Their Influence in the Marketplace," *AdWeek*, February 27, 2012. Available at: http://www.adweek.com/sa-article/bread-buyer-and-breadwinner-138545.

11 Kay and Shipman, p. 14.

12 "Women in Senior Management: Setting the Stage for Growth," Grant Thorton International Business Report, 2013. p. 2. Available at: http://www.gti.org/files/ibr2013_wib_report_final.pdf. Also, "The Bottom Line: Connecting Corporate Performance and Gender Diversity," Catalyst, 2004. Availalbe at: http://www.catalyst.org/knowledge/bottom-line-connecting-corporate-performance-and-gender-diversity.

13 Ann Friedman, "Tech Women Are Busy Building Their Own Networks," *Washington Post*, January 9, 2014. Available at: http://www.washingtonpost.com/lifestyle/style/tech-women-are-busy-building-their-own-networks/2014/01/08/60e356f2-7874-11e3-af7f-13bf0e9965f6_story.html.

14 Telework Research Network. Available at: http://www.teleworkresearchnetwork.com/telecommuting-statistics.

15 Global Workplace Analytics.com; Rachel Emma Silverman, "Stuck at Home: 10 Tips for Working," *Wall Street Journal*, November 2, 2012.

16 Wendy Wang, Kim Parker, and Paul Taylor, "Breadwinner Moms," Pew Research Center, May 29, 2013, p.4. Available at: http://www.pewsocialtrends.org/files/2013/05/Breadwinner_moms_final.pdf.

17 Paul Taylor, Kim Parker, Rich Morin, Eileen Pratten, and, Anna Brown, "Millenials in Adulthood: Detached From Institutions, Networked

with Friends," Pew Research Center, March 7, 2014 p. 10. http://www.pewsocialtrends.org/files/2014/03/2014-03-07_generations-report-version-for-web.pdf.

18   Department of Labor. See: http://www.dol.gov/equalpay/.

19   June O'Neill, "The Gender Gap in Wages, Circa 2000," *American Economic Review 93*, no. 2, 2003, pp. 309-314.

20   "An Analysis of Reasons for the Disparity in Wages Between Men and Women," CONSAD Research Group, prepared for the Department of Labor, January 12, 2009, p. 1.

21   "Why Women Make Less Than Men," Kay Hymowitz, *Wall Street Journal*, April 26, 2012.

22   Belinda Luscombe, "Workplace Salaries: At Last, Women On Top," *Time Magazine*, September 1, 2010; Carrie Lukas, "There Is No Male-Female Wage Gap," *Wall Street Journal*, April 11, 2011.

23   See proposed legislation here: http://beta.congress.gov/bill/113th-congress/senate-bill/84.

24   For more information on the FAMILY Act, see IWF's Policy Focus here: http://c1355372.cdn.cloudfiles.rackspacecloud.com/167e75a7-d65b-4c41-8b1a-14570e2268b1/PolicyFocus14_Jan_p1.pdf.

25   "2013 Working Mother 100 Best Companies," *Working Mother*. Available at: http://www.workingmother.com/best-companies.

26   "100 Best Companies," *Working Mother*, 2013. Available at: http://www.workingmother.com/best-company-list/146788?page=1.

27   Kay and Shipman, 204-206.

CHAPTER 5

1   U.S. Department of Education, National Center for Education Statistics, *The Condition of Education 2009*, Indicator 32, p. 72. Available at: http://nces.ed.gov/pubs2009/2009081.pdf.

2   Caroline M. Hoxby, "Does Competition among Public Schools Benefit Students and Taxpayers?" *The American Economic Review,* vol. 90, no. 5 (December 2000): 1209; Hoxby, *School Choice and School Productivity (or Could School Choice be a Tide that Lifts All Boats?),* National Bureau of Economic Research, Working Paper 8873, April 2002, p. 50.

3   The original per-pupil funding amount of $2,490 in 2000 dollars was adjusted to reflect 2014 inflation-adjusted dollars, $3,394.92. See Jay P. Greene, "2001 Education Freedom Index," Civic Report 24, January 2002, p. 8. Available at: http://www.manhattan-institute.org/html/cr_24.htm.

4   The original median household income figure of $6,405 in 2000 dollars was adjusted to reflect 2014 inflation-adjusted dollars, $8,732.71. See Jay P. Greene, "2001 Education Freedom Index," Civic Report 24, January 2002, p. 8. Available at: http://www.manhattan-institute.org/html/cr_24.htm.

5   Caroline M. Hoxby, *School Choice and School Productivity (or Could School Choice be a Tide that Lifts All Boats?),* National Bureau of Economic Research, Working Paper 8873, April 2002, pp. 22-28, especially pp. 27-78, p. 50, and Table III, p. 59. For a non-technical version see, "Rising Tide," *Education Next*, Winter 2001, pp. 68-74. Available at: http://www.hoover.org/publications/ednext/3399061.html.

6   National Alliance for Public Charter Schools, Funding. Available at: http://dashboard.publiccharters.org/dashboard/policy/page/funding/year/2010.

7   Vicki E. Murray (Alger), *Empowering Teachers with Choice: How a Diversified Education System Benefits Teachers, Students, and America*, Independent

Women's Forum, Policy Paper No. 605, July 2007. Available at: http://www. iwf.org/files/dea58ae33799f48b2699de31cc5e3e35.pdf.

8   National Alliance for Public Charter Schools, "Estimated Number of Public Charter Schools & Students," 2013-2014, February 2014. Available at: http:// www.publiccharters.org/wp-content/uploads/2014/02/New-and-Closed-Report-February-20141.pdf.

9   National Conference of State Legislatures, Parent Trigger Laws in the States. Available at: http://www.ncsl.org/research/education/state-parent-trigger-laws.aspx.

10   Home School Legal Defense Association, Academic Statistics on Homeschooling. Available at: http://www.hslda.org/docs/ nche/000010/200410250.asp; and "Progress Report 2009: Homeschool Academic Achievement and Demographics," Home School Legal Defense Association. Available at: http://www.hslda.org/docs/study/ray2009/2009_Ray_StudyFINAL.pdf.

11   Friedman Foundation for Educational Choice, "Types of School Choice," *ABCs of School Choice 2014 Edition*. Available at: http://www.edchoice. org/School-Choice/The-ABCs-of-School-Choice/ABCs-Blue/Types-of-School-Choice-Programs-and-Schooling-Opti; and John Watson, Amy Murin, Lauren Vashaw, Butch Gemin, and Chris Rapp, *Keeping Pace with K-12 Online and Blended Learning*, October 2013. Available at: http://kpk12.com/ cms/wp-content/uploads/EEG_KP2013-lr.pdf.

12   Vicki E. Alger, *The Vital Need for Virtual Schools in Nebraska, Platte Institute for Economic Research*, June 2011. Available at: https://www.platteinstitute. org/Library/docLib/20110623_my_Virtual_Schools_policy_report2.pdf; Lance T. Izumi and Vicki E. Murray (Alger), *Short Circuited: The Challenges Facing the Online Learning Revolution in California* (San Francisco: Pacific Research Institute, 2011). Available at: http://www.pacificresearch.org/ docLib/20110113_shortcircuited_r5%284%29.pdf.

13   The American Center for School Choice, Assembling the Evidence, Schools Available at: http://assemblingtheevidence.org/schools/index.jsp; and Students. Available at: http://assemblingtheevidence.org/students/index.jsp.

14   "U.S. voucher, school choice enrollment reaches record high" Freidman Foundation for Educational Choice Press Release, January 23, 2014. Available at: http://www.edchoice.org/Newsroom/News/U-S—voucher--school-choice-enrollment-reaches-record-high.aspx.

15   Friedman Foundation for Educational Choice, *ABCs of School Choice 2014 Edition*. Available at: http://www.edchoice.org/CMSModules/EdChoice/ FileLibrary/965/The-ABCs-of-School-Choice---2013-edition.pdf.

16   The American Federation for Children, *School Choice Yearbook, 2012-13*. Available at: http://www.allianceforschoolchoice.org/yearbook; and Facts. Available at: http://www.federationforchildren.org/facts.

17   "U.S. voucher, school choice enrollment reaches record high" Freidman Foundation for Educational Choice Press Release, January 23, 2014. Available at: http://www.edchoice.org/Newsroom/News/U-S—voucher--school-choice-enrollment-reaches-record-high.aspx. And the American Federation for Children, *School Choice Yearbook, 2012-13*, p. 30. Available at: http://www.allianceforschoolchoice.org/yearbook. Timeline of Educational Choice. Available at: http://s3.amazonaws.com/assets. allianceforschoolchoice.com/admin_assets/uploads/138/Timeline%20 of%20Educational%20Choice.pdf.

18   Friedman Foundation for Educational Choice, Gold Standard Studies. Available at: http://www.edchoice.org/Research/Gold-Standard-Studies. aspx. Greg Forster, *A Win-Win Solution: The Empirical Evidence on School*

Choice, Friedman Foundation for Educational Choice, April 17, 2013. Available at: http://www.edchoice.org/Research/Reports/A-Win-Win-Solution—The-Empirical-Evidence-on-School-Choice.aspx. Institute for Justice, School Choice. Available at: http://www.ij.org/cases/schoolchoice. American Federation for Children, *School Choice Yearbook, 2012-13*, pp. 24-25. Available at: http://www.allianceforschoolchoice.org/yearbook. Faces of Educational Choice. Available at: http://s3.amazonaws.com/assets. allianceforschoolchoice.com/admin_assets/uploads/160/The%20Faces%20 of%20Educational%20Choice.pdf.

19   Friedman Foundation for Educational Choice, School Choice Programs. Available at: http://www.edchoice.org/School-Choice/School-Choice-Programs.

20   Institute for Justice, *Zelman v. Simmons-Harris*. Available at: http://www. ij.org/zelman-v-simmons-harris. Friedman Foundation for Education Choice, Vermont. Available at: http://www.edchoice.org/School-Choice/Programs/Town-Tuitioning-Program-1.aspx. Maine. Available at: http://www.edchoice. org/School-Choice/Programs/Town-Tuitioning-Program.aspx.

21   For a research summary, see Vicki E. Alger, *Faith-based Schools: Their Contributions to American Education, Society, and the Economy: Final Report to the Commission on Faith-based Schools*, American Center for School Choice, November 2013, pp. 25-27 and 32-33. Available at: http://www.amcsc.org/publications/Final-Report_Assembling-the-Evidence.pdf.

22   Vicki E. Alger, "Distinction with a Difference: Tax Credit Scholarships are Not Vouchers," IWF Inkwell Blog, February 2, 2010. Available at: http://www.iwf. org/blog/2430508/Distinction-with-a-Difference:-Tax-Credit-Scholarships-are-Not-Vouchers.

23   Institute for Justice, *Arizona Christian School Tuition Organization v. Winn.* Available at: http://www.ij.org/arizona-school-choice-release-4-4-11.

24   Friedman Foundation for Educational Choice, School Choice Programs. Available at: http://www.edchoice.org/School-Choice/School-Choice-Programs; and American Federation for Children, "Types of School Choice Programs," *School Choice Yearbook, 2012-13*, pp. 9-10. Available at: http://www.allianceforschoolchoice.org/yearbook. Direct link: http:// s3.amazonaws.com/assets.allianceforschoolchoice.com/admin_assets/uploads/132/Types%20of%20School%20Choice%20Programs.pdf.

25   For a research summary, see Vicki E. Alger, *Faith-based Schools: Their Contributions to American Education, Society, and the Economy: Final Report to the Commission on Faith-based Schools*, and the *Economy: Final Report to the Commission on Faith-based Schools*, American Center for School Choice, November 2013, pp. 29-31. Available at: http://www.amcsc.org/publications/Final-Report_Assembling-the-Evidence. pdf. See also Assembling the Evidence, Funding. Available at: http://assemblingtheevidence.org/funding/index.jsp.

26   Friedman Foundation for Educational Choice, Arizona Empowerment Scholarship Accounts. Available at: http://www.edchoice.org/School-Choice/Programs/Empowerment-Scholarship-Accounts.aspx.

27   Andrew Ujifusa, "Arizona Supreme Court: School-Choice Savings Accounts Can Continue," *Education Week*, March 24, 2014. Available at: http://blogs. edweek.org/edweek/state_edwatch/2014/03/arizona_supreme_court_school-choice_savings_accounts_can_continue.html.

28   Brittany Corona, "Education Savings Accounts Deemed Constitutional by Arizona Supreme Court," The Heritage Foundation Foundry, March 21, 2014. Available at: http://blog.heritage.org/2014/03/21/education-savings-accounts-deemed-constitutional-arizona-supreme-court/; and Andrew

Ujifusa, "Arizona Supreme Court: School-Choice Savings Accounts Can Continue," *Education Week*, March 24, 2014. Available at: http://blogs. edweek.org/edweek/state_edwatch/2014/03/arizona_supreme_court_ school-choice_savings_accounts_can_continue.html.

29   Lloyd Bentsen IV, "Oklahoma Wants to be Next," National Center for Policy Analysis, February 6, 2014. Available at: http://educationblog.ncpa.org/ oklahoma-wants-to-be-next/; and Joy Pullman, "Oklahoma may become second state to offer students education savings accounts," EAG News, January 30, 2014. Available at: http://eagnews.org/oklahoma-may-become-second-state-to-offer-education-savings-accounts/.

30   Vicki E. Alger, "A Candid Look at Common Core," IWF Policy Focus, November 17, 2013. Available at: http://www.iwf.org/publications/2792553/ Policy-Focus:-A-Candid-Look-at-Common-Core-; and "Time to Retire, Not Reauthorize, No Child Left Behind," IWF Policy Focus, July 18, 2013. Available at: http://www.iwf.org/publications/2791754/Time-to-Retire,-Not-Reauthorize,-No-Child-Left-Behind.

31   Project on Student Debt. Available at: http://projectonstudentdebt.org/.

32   Josh Mitchell and Maya Jackson-Randall, "Student Loan Debt Tops $1 Trillion," *Wall Street Journal*, March 22, 2012; "Could $1T student loan debt derail U.S. recovery?" CBS News, April 4, 2012. Available at: http://www.cbsnews.com/ news/could-1t-student-loan-debt-derail-us-recovery/. Terry Savage, "Recent grads must face up to student loan debt," *Chicago Sun-Times*, October 26, 2011. Available at: http://www.suntimes.com/business/savage/8435699-452/ recent-grads-must-face-up-to-student-loan-debt.html.

33   Elvina Nawaguna, "Jobs become more elusive for recent U.S. college grads -NY Fed," Reuters, January 6, 2014. Available at: http://www.reuters.com/ article/2014/01/06/usa-studentloans-jobs-idUSL2N0KG1SW20140106. Patrice Hill, "College grads find big degree of debt, difficulty," *Washington Times*, July 5, 2012. Available at: http://www.washingtontimes.com/ news/2012/jul/5/college-grads-find-big-degree-of-debt-difficulty/.

34   Jaison R. Abel, Richard Deitz, and Yaqin Su, "Are Recent College Graduates Finding Good Jobs?" Federal Reserve Bank of New York, *Current Issues in Economics and Finance*, Vol. 20, No. 1, 2014, pp. 3-4. Available at: http:// www.newyorkfed.org/research/current_issues/ci20-1.pdf.

35   Shahien Nasiripour and Chris Kirkham, "Student Loan Defaults Surge To Highest Level In Nearly 2 Decades," *Huffington Post*, September 30, 2013. Available at: http://www.huffingtonpost.com/2013/09/30/student-loans-default_n_4019806.html.

36   Vicki E. Alger, "Student Loans and College Affordability," IWF Policy Focus, August 7, 2012. Available at: http://www.iwf.org/publications/2788735/ Student-Loans-and-College-Affordability; and "Obama's college affordability scheme gets an 'F'," *Washington Examiner*, September 7, 2013. Available at: http://washingtonexaminer.com/obamas-college-affordability-scheme-gets-an-f/article/2535358.

37   Vicki E. Alger, "Making College Affordable," *The Star Tribune* (Minneapolis), August 9, 2012. Available at: http://iwf.org/news/2788779/; "Athletic/ Instruction Expenditures," Center for College Affordability and Productivity. Available at: http://centerforcollegeaffordability.org/data/sports-spending-data; Steve Cohen, "Oh, So That's Why College is So Expensive," *Forbes*, August 28, 2012. Available at: http://www.forbes.com/sites/ stevecohen/2012/08/28/oh-so-thats-why-college-is-so-expensive/; and Laura A. Bischoff, "OSU president expenses in the millions," *Dayton Daily News*, September 22, 2012. Available at: http://www.daytondailynews.com/

news/news/state-regional-govt-politics/expenses-of-osu-president-run-into-millions-for-tr/nSGkK/.

38 Quoted in Allysia Finley, "Richard Vedder: The Real Reason College Costs So Much," *Wall Street Journal*, August 26, 2013. Available at: http://online.wsj.com/news/articles/SB10001424127887324619504579029282438522674.

39 Jay P. Greene, "Administrative Bloat at American Universities: The Real Reason for High Costs in Higher Education," Goldwater Institute Policy Report No. 239, August 17, 2010. Available at: http://goldwaterinstitute.org/article/administrative-bloat-american-universities-real-reason-high-costs-higher-education.

40 Vicki Alger, "State of the Union 2012—Situation Normal: All Fed-Ed Up," IWF Blog, January 26, 2012. Available at: http://www.iwf.org/blog/2786804/State-of-the-Union-2012---Situation-Normal:-All-Fed-Ed-Up.

41 Vicki E. Alger, "Student Loans and College Affordability," IWF Policy Focus, August 7, 2012. Available at: http://www.iwf.org/publications/2788735/Student-Loans-and-College-Affordability; and "Making College Affordable," *The Star Tribune* (Minneapolis), August 9, 2012. Available at: http://iwf.org/news/2788779/.

42 Neal McCluskey, "Our Greedy Colleges," Cato Institute, Cato at Liberty Blog, June 15, 2012. Available at: http://www.cato.org/blog/our-greedy-colleges.

43 Robert E. Martin and Andrew Gillen, "How College Pricing Undermines Financial Aid," Center for College Affordability and Productivity blog, March 2011. Available at: http://centerforcollegeaffordability.org/research/studies/college-pricing-and-financial-aid; and Table 3, p. 9 of full study. Available at: http://centerforcollegeaffordability.org/uploads/How_College_Pricing_Undermines.pdf.

44 U.S. Chamber of Commerce, Leaders & Laggards: A State-by-State Report Card on Public Postsecondary Education. Available at: http://education.uschamber.com/reportcard/efficiency-cost-effectiveness/; and Pew Research Center, "College Graduation: Weighing the Cost … and the Payoff," May 17, 2012. Available at: http://www.pewresearch.org/2012/05/17/college-graduation-weighing-the-cost-and-the-payoff/.

45 Richard Arum and Josipa Roksa, "Are Undergraduates Actually Learning Anything?" *Chronicle of Higher Education*, January 18, 2011. Available at: http://chronicle.com/article/Are-Undergraduates-Actually/125979/.

46 "Gov. Perry: We Must Reform, Streamline State Government," Office of the Governor Rick Perry, February 8, 2011. Available at: http://governor.state.tx.us/news/speech/15673/; cf. Ross Ramsey, "Perry to Push Texas Colleges to Offer $10,000 Degree," *The Texas Tribune*, February 8, 2011. Available at: http://www.texastribune.org/2011/02/08/perry-to-push-texas-colleges-to-offer-10000-degree/; and Lara Seligman, "Does Texas Have an Answer to Sky-High Tuition?" *National Journal*, November 23, 2012. Available at: http://news.yahoo.com/does-texas-answer-sky-high-tuition-060005341—politics.html.

47 "Gov. Rick Perry Applauds Efforts to Improve Affordability at Texas Tech University System and University of Houston System," Office of the Governor Rick Perry, May 17, 2013, Press Release. Available at: http://governor.state.tx.us/news/press-release/18529/.

48 "The Truth-o-Meter Says: "13 Texas universities "have announced or implemented a $10,000 degree','" *Austin American-Statesman PolitiFact Texas*, May 31, 2013. Available at: http://www.politifact.com/texas/statements/2013/may/31/rick-perry/rick-perry-says-13-texas-universities-have-announc/.

49 Sammy Mack, "Update: Shaky Start To $10,000 College Degree Programs in Florida," *State Impact*, NPR, October 14, 2013. Available at: https://stateimpact.npr.org/florida/2013/10/14/update-shaky-start-to-10000-college-degree-programs-in-florida/.

50 National Governors Association, "The Governors Speak, 2014," NGA Paper, March 13, 2014. Available at: http://www.nga.org/files/live/sites/NGA/files/pdf/2014/1403TheGovernorsSpeak.pdf.

51 Richard Vedder, "How the $10,000 Plan Might Work," *New York Times*, October 26, 2011. Available at: http://www.nytimes.com/roomfordebate/2011/09/05/rick-perrys-plan-10000-for-a-ba/how-the-texas-plan-might-work.

52 Vicki E. Alger, "Let Students and Their Families Rate Colleges Themselves," IWF Blog, August 24, 2013. Available at: http://www.iwf.org/blog/2791982/Let-Students-and-their-Families-Rate-Colleges-Themselves-; and "Obama's college affordability scheme gets an 'F'," *Washington Examiner*, September 7, 2013. Available at: http://washingtonexaminer.com/obamas-college-affordability-scheme-gets-an-f/article/2535358.

53 Richard Vedder, *Going Broke by Degree: Why College Costs Too Much* (Washington, DC: AEI Press, 2004), pp. 79-88.

54 Vicki Murray (Alger), *The Privately Financed Public University: A Case Study of the University of Michigan*, Goldwater Institute Policy Report No. 206, November 1, 2005. Available at: http://heartland.org/sites/all/modules/custom/heartland_migration/files/pdfs/19150.pdf.

55 Vicki Murray (Alger), *Cash for College: Bringing Free-market Reform to Higher Education*, Goldwater Institute Policy Report No. 208, March 14, 2006. Available at: http://heartland.org/sites/all/modules/custom/heartland_migration/files/pdfs/19145.pdf.

CHAPTER 6

1 Vicki E. Alger, "Universal Government Preschool: Still Waiting for Promised Payoffs Decades Later," IWF Blog, February 14, 2014. Available at: http://www.iwf.org/blog/2793079/Universal-Government-Preschool:-Still-Waiting-for-Promised-Payoffs-Decades-Later; "Mr. Preschool President," IWF Blog, February 15, 2013, http://iwf.org/blog/2790567/; and "Keep Uncle Sam out of Preschool," *Boston Herald*, September 29, 2013. Available at: http://www.iwf.org/news/2792203/Keep-Uncle-Sam-Out-of-Preschool.

2 Vicki E. Alger, "Universal Government Preschool: Still Waiting for Promised Payoffs Decades Later," IWF Blog, February 14, 2014. Available at: http://www.iwf.org/blog/2793079/Universal-Government-Preschool:-Still-Waiting-for-Promised-Payoffs-Decades-Later.

3 "Early Learning: America's Middle Class Promise Begins Early," U.S. Department of Education. Available at: https://www.ed.gov/early-learning.

4 Vicki E. Alger, "Saying No to Government Preschool," IWF Policy Focus, September 12, 2013. Available at: http://iwf.org/publications/2792115/.

5 Vicki E. Alger, "Saying No to Government Preschool," IWF Policy Focus, September 12, 2013. Available at: http://iwf.org/publications/2792115/; "Mr. Preschool President," IWF Blog, February 15, 2013. Available at: http://iwf.org/blog/2790567/; and "Early Learning: America's Middle Class Promise Begins Early," U.S. Department of Education. Available at: https://www.ed.gov/early-learning.

6 Vicki E. Alger, "Saying No to Government Preschool," IWF Policy Focus, September 12, 2013. Available at: http://iwf.org/publications/2792115/.

7 *Ibid.*

8   *Ibid.*
9   Lynda Laughlin, "Who's Minding the Kids? Child Care Arrangements: Spring 2011," U.S. Census Bureau, Household Economic Studies, P70-135, April 2013, Table 3, p. 9, and p. 22. Available at: http://www.census.gov/prod/2013pubs/p70-135.pdf.
10   Tran D. Keys, George Farkas, Margaret R. Burchinal, Greg J. Duncan, Deborah L. Vandell, Weilin Li, Erik A. Ruzek, and Carollee Howes, "Preschool Center Quality and School Readiness: Quality Effects and Variation by Demographic and Child Characteristics," *Child Development*, Vol. 84, Issue 4 (July/August 2013), pp. 1171-1190. Available at: http://onlinelibrary.wiley.com/doi/10.1111/cdev.12048/abstract; Janet I. Jacob, "The socio-emotional effects of non-maternal childcare on children in the USA: a critical review of recent studies," *Early Child Development and Care*, Vol. 179, Issue 5 (July 7, 2009), pp. 559-70. Available at: http://www.tandfonline.com/doi/abs/10.1080/03004430701292988#.Uzrw71fT6K5; Susanna Loeb, Margaret Bridges, Bruce Fuller, Russ Rumberger, Daphna Bassok, "How Much is Too Much? The Influence of Preschool Centers on Children's Social and Cognitive Development," *Economics of Education Review*, Vol. 26, No.1 (February 2007), pp. 52-66. Available at: http://www.nber.org/papers/w11812; Lisa A. McCabe and Ellen C. Frede, "Challenging Behaviors and the Role of Preschool Education," National Institute for Early Education Research (NIEER) Policy Brief, Issue 16, December 2007. Available at: http://www.nieer.org/resources/policybriefs/16.pdf; Michael Baker, Jonathan Gruber, and Kevin Milligan, "What Can We Learn from Quebec's Universal Childcare Program?" C.D. Howe Institute, February 2006. Available at: http://www.cdhowe.org/pdf/ebrief_25_english.pdf; National Institute of Child Health and Human Development (NICHD) Early Child Care Research Network, "Does Amount of Time Spent in Child Care Predict Socio-emotional Adjustment During the Transition to Kindergarten?" *Child Development*, Vol. 74, Issue 4 (July/August 2003), pp. 976-1005. Available at: http://onlinelibrary.wiley.com/doi/10.1111/1467-8624.00582/abstract; David Elkind, *Miseducation: Preschoolers at Risk* (New York: Alfred A. Knopf, 1987); and Ron Haskins, "Public School Aggression among Children with Varying Day-Care Experiences," *Child Development*, Vol., 56, No. 3 (June 1985), pp. 689-703. Available at: http://www.jstor.org/discover/10.2307/1129759?uid=3739552&uid=2129&uid=2&uid=70&uid=4&uid=3739256&sid=21103907111513.
11   Carrie Lukas, "Keep Uncle Sam Away from Toddlers: The Case Against Government Preschool," IWF Policy Brief #22, June 11, 2009. Available at: http://www.iwf.org/files/ccd51591aa7467a111d9f4437830ea9c.pdf; and "Early Child Care and Education Philosophies," Columbia University Work Life School and Child Care Service, Fall 2011. Available at: http://worklife.columbia.edu/files_worklife/public/Early_Child_Care_Philosophies_8_25_11.pdf.
12   Louise Stoney, Pam Tatum, and Carla Hibbard, "Shared Services for the ECE Industry: A New Approach to Finance and Management," Child Care Aware of America Thought Forum on ECE Finance, April 12, 2013, p. 2. Available at: http://www.naccrra.org/sites/default/files/default_site_pages/2013/shared_services_pptfinal.pdf.
13   The conference was at George Washington University School of Medicine on April 17, 1997. The remarks of Stanley I. Greenspan are quoted from, "Changing Our Thinking About Child Care: Even The Best Of Day-care Centers Can't Offer What Infants Ultimately Need The Most - Parental Care," Special to *The Washington Post*, published in the *Orlando Sentinel*,

November 9, 1997. Available at: http://articles.orlandosentinel.com/1997-11-09/news/9711070902_1_parental-care-day-care-out-of-home-care.

14   U.S. Department of Health and Human Services, Administration for Children and Families, Office of Head Start, History of Head Start. Available at: http://www.acf.hhs.gov/programs/ohs/about/history-of-head-start; Head Start of Lane County, History of Head Start. Available at: http://www.hsolc.org/content/history-head-start-program; Head Start Program Facts Fiscal Year 2012. Available at: http://eclkc.ohs.acf.hhs.gov/hslc/mr/factsheets/2012-hs-program-factsheet.html; and Head Start Report to the House Ways and Means Committee, p. 1, Table 15-33. Available at: http://waysandmeans.house.gov/media/pdf/110/head.pdf.

15   Head Start Impact Study and Follow-up, 2000-2013, http://www.acf.hhs.gov/programs/opre/research/project/head-start-impact-study-and-follow-up. See Michael Puma, Stephen Bell, Ronna Cook, and Camilla Heid, *Head Start Impact Study Final Report*, Prepared for: Office of Planning, Research and Evaluation, Administration for Children and Families, U.S. Department of Health and Human Services, January 2010, pp. p. 3-51, 9-3 and 9-4. Available at: http://www.acf.hhs.gov/sites/default/files/opre/hs_impact_study_final.pdf; and Michael Puma, Stephen Bell, Ronna Cook, Camilla Heid, Pam Broene, and Frank Jenkins, Andrew Mashburn, and Jason Downer, *Third Grade Follow-up to the Head Start Impact Study Final Report*, October 2012, pp. xvii, xxii, 92, and 147. Available at: http://www.acf.hhs.gov/sites/default/files/opre/head_start_report.pdf.

16   Vicki E. Alger, "Mr. Preschool President," IWF Blog, February 15, 2013. Available at: http://iwf.org/blog/2790567/.

17   Casey Given, "President Obama's $75 Billion Dollar Preschool Bluff," *Forbes*, February 7, 2014. Available at: http://www.forbes.com/sites/realspin/2014/02/07/president-obamas-75-billion-dollar-preschool-bluff/; Carrie Lukas, "Keep Uncle Sam Away from Toddlers: The Case Against Government Preschool," IWF Policy Brief #22, June 11, 2009, p. 3. Available at: http://www.iwf.org/files/ccd51591aa7467a111d9f4437830ea9c.pdf; Adam B. Schaeffer, "The Poverty of Preschool Promises: Saving Children and Money with the Early Education Tax Credit," Cato Institute Policy Analysis No. 641, August 3, 2009, pp. 2-3. Available at: http://www.cato.org/publications/policy-analysis/poverty-preschool-promises-saving-children-money-early-education-tax-credit; and Darcy Olsen, "Assessing Proposals for Preschool and Kindergarten: Essential Information for Parents, Taxpayers, and Policymakers," Goldwater Institute Policy Report No. 201, February 8, 2005, pp. 18-21. Available at: http://goldwaterinstitute.org/sites/default/files/Assessing%20Proposals%20for%20Preschool%20and%20Kindergarten.pdf.

18   Quotation from Kenneth T. Walsh, "The Three R's and the Big P," *U.S. News & World Report*, August 30, 1999. Cited in Darcy Olsen, "Assessing Proposals for Preschool and Kindergarten: Essential Information for Parents, Taxpayers, and Policymakers," Goldwater Institute Policy Report No. 201, February 8, 2005, p. 5. Available at: http://goldwaterinstitute.org/sites/default/files/Assessing%20Proposals%20for%20Preschool%20and%20Kindergarten.pdf.

19   Adam B. Schaeffer, "The Poverty of Preschool Promises: Saving Children and Money with the Early Education Tax Credit," Cato Institute Policy Analysis No. 641, August 3, 2009, pp. 3-4. Available at: http://www.cato.org/publications/policy-analysis/poverty-preschool-promises-saving-children-money-early-education-tax-credit; and Darcy Olsen, "Assessing Proposals for Preschool and Kindergarten: Essential Information for Parents,

Taxpayers, and Policymakers," Goldwater Institute Policy Report No. 201, February 8, 2005, pp. 21-23. Available at: http://goldwaterinstitute.org/sites/default/files/Assessing%20Proposals%20for%20Preschool%20and%20Kindergarten.pdf.

20 Adam B. Schaeffer, "The Poverty of Preschool Promises: Saving Children and Money with the Early Education Tax Credit," Cato Institute Policy Analysis No. 641, August 3, 2009, pp. 4-5. Available at: http://www.cato.org/publications/policy-analysis/poverty-preschool-promises-saving-children-money-early-education-tax-credit.

21 Lynn A. Karoly and James H. Bigelow, *The Economics of Investing in Universal Preschool Education in California*, RAND Corporation, 2005, pp. xiv, xxxvi, 96, 112, and 141. Available at: http://www.rand.org/content/dam/rand/pubs/monographs/2005/RAND_MG349.pdf; and U.S. Department of Health and Human Services, "High-Quality Preschool Program Produces Long-Term Economic Payoff," National Institutes for Health News, February 4, 2011. Available at: http://www.nih.gov/news/health/feb2011/nichd-04.htm.

22 Arthur J. Reynolds, Judy A. Temple, Dylan L. Robertson, and Emily A. Mann, "Long-term Effects of an Early Childhood Intervention on Educational Achievement and Juvenile Arrest: A 15-Year Follow-up of Low-Income Children in Public Schools," *Journal of the American Medical Association*, Vol. 285, No. 18 (May 9, 2001), pp. 2339-2346. Available at: http://jama.jamanetwork.com/article.aspx?articleid=193816.

23 Nicholas Kristof, "Pre-K, The Great Debate," *New York Times*, January 29, 2014. Available at: http://www.nytimes.com/2014/01/30/opinion/kristof-pre-k-the-great-debate.html?_r=0.

24 Vicki E. Alger, "Universal Government Preschool: Still Waiting for Promised Payoffs Decades Later," IWF Blog, February 14, 2014. Available at: http://www.iwf.org/blog/2793079/Universal-Government-Preschool:-Still-Waiting-for-Promised-Payoffs-Decades-Later; and Dylan Matthews, "James Heckman: In Early Education, Quality Really Matters," *Washington Post* Wonk Blog, February 14, 2013. Available at: http://www.washingtonpost.com/blogs/wonkblog/wp/2013/02/14/james-heckman-in-early-childhood-education-quality-really-matters/.

25 Child Care Aware of America, *Parents and the High Costs of Child Care*, 2013 Report, p. 14. Available at: http://usa.childcareaware.org/sites/default/files/cost_of_care_2013_103113_0.pdf.

26 Lynda Laughlin, "Who's Minding the Kids? Child Care Arrangements: Spring 2011," U.S. Census Bureau, Household Economic Studies, P70-135, April 2013, pp. 14 and 19. Available at: http://www.census.gov/prod/2013pubs/p70-135.pdf.

27 Bill Bischoff, "Child-care Tax Breaks for Working Parents," *Market Watch*, March 6, 2013. Available at: http://www.marketwatch.com/story/child-care-tax-breaks-for-working-parents-2013-03-06; and Kimberly Lankford, "Tax Breaks for Child-Care Expenses," *Kiplinger*, March 20, 2014. Available at: http://www.kiplinger.com/article/taxes/T054-C001-S003-tax-breaks-for-child-care-expenses.html.

28 Kimberly Lankford, "FSA or Child-Care Credit?" *Kiplinger*, October 13, 2010. Available at: http://www.kiplinger.com/article/taxes/T055-C001-S001-fsa-or-child-care-credit.html; and "Tax Breaks for Child-Care Expenses," *Kiplinger*, March 20, 2014. Available at: http://www.kiplinger.com/article/taxes/T054-C001-S003-tax-breaks-for-child-care-expenses.html.

29 W. Steven Barnett, Megan E. Carolan, Jen Fitzgerald, and James H. Squires, *The State of Preschool 2012: State Preschool Yearbook*, National Institute for Early Education Research (NIEER), 2012, p. 7. Available at: http://nieer.org/sites/nieer/files/yearbook2012.pdf.

30   Cynthia G. Brown, Donna Cooper, Juliana Herman, Melissa Lazarín, Michael
      Linden, Sasha Post, and Neera Tanden, "Investing in Our Children: A Plan
      to Expand Access to Preschool and Child Care," February 6, 2013, p. 3.
      Available at: http://www.scribd.com/doc/124185683/Investing-in-Our-
      Children-A-Plan-to-Expand-Access-to-Preschool-and-Child-Care.

31   Vicki E. Alger, "SOTU 2014: D.C.-Driven Preschool Redux," IWF Blog,
      January 28, 2014. Available at: http://iwf.org/blog/2793030/SOTU-2014:-
      D.C.-Driven-Preschool-Redux; and "Obama's Underperforming Preschool
      Plan," *Washington Times*, February 27, 2013. Available at: http://iwf.org/
      news/2790663/.

32   Adam B. Schaeffer, "The Poverty of Preschool Promises: Saving Children
      and Money with the Early Education Tax Credit," Cato Institute Policy
      Analysis No. 641, August 3, 2009, pp. 2-3. Available at: http://www.cato.org/
      publications/policy-analysis/poverty-preschool-promises-saving-children-
      money-early-education-tax-credit.

33   Greg Corombos, "Real Unemployment Rate is 11%," World Net Daily,
      March 9, 2014. Available at: http://www.wnd.com/2014/03/economist-
      real-unemployment-rate-is-11/; Ben Berkowitz, "Chart: What's the real
      unemployment rate?" NBR, CNBC.com, March 7, 2014. Available at: http://
      nbr.com/2014/03/07/chart-whats-the-real-unemployment-rate-2/; cf. U.S.
      Department of Labor, Bureau of Labor Statistics, Employment Situation
      Summary, March 7, 2014. Available at: http://www.bls.gov/news.release/
      empsit.nr0.htm. See "U-6 Total unemployed, plus all persons marginally
      attached to the labor force, plus total employed part time for economic
      reasons, as a percent of the civilian labor force plus all persons marginally
      attached to the labor force" in Table A-15. Alternative measures of labor
      underutilization. Available at: http://www.bls.gov/news.release/empsit.t15.
      htm. For debt figure, see Treasury Direct, The Debt to the Penny and Who
      Holds It. Available at: http://www.treasurydirect.gov/NP/debt/current.

34   U.S. Department of Education, *Digest of Education Statistics 2012*, Table
      35. Available at: http://nces.ed.gov/programs/digest/d12/tables/dt12_035.
      asp; and Vicki E. Alger, "Blame Monopolies—Not Private School Moms and
      Dads—for Bad Public Schools," IWF Blog, August 29, 2013. Available at:
      http://www.iwf.org/blog/2792035/Blame-Monopolies%E2%80%94Not-
      Private-School-Moms-and-Dads%E2%80%94for-Bad-Public-Schools.

35   Neal McCluskey, "Educational Outcomes Have Not Improved" in
      K-12 Subsidies, Cato Institute, May 2009. Available at: http://www.
      downsizinggovernment.org/education/k-12-education-subsidies#Rising.

36   "U.S. Voucher, School Choice Enrollment Reaches Record High" Freidman
      Foundation for Educational Choice Press Release, January 23, 2014.
      Available at: http://www.edchoice.org/Newsroom/News/U-S--voucher-
      -school-choice-enrollment-reaches-record-high.aspx; and the American
      Federation for Children, *School Choice Yearbook, 2012-13*, p. 30. Available
      at: http://www.allianceforschoolchoice.org/yearbook. Timeline of
      Educational Choice. Available at: http://s3.amazonaws.com/assets.
      allianceforschoolchoice.com/admin_assets/uploads/138/Timeline%20
      of%20Educational%20Choice.pdf.

37   Friedman Foundation for Educational Choice, "Does School Choice Have a
      Positive Academic Impact on Participating Students?" Available at: http://
      www.edchoice.org/getattachment/School-Choice/School-Choice-FAQs/
      Does-school-choice-have-a-positive-academic-impact-on-participating-
      students.pdf.

CHAPTER 7

1   Kellyanne Conway, "National Online Survey of Women on 'Alarmism'," The polling company, inc./WomanTrend, Washington, D.C. May 17, 2013.

2   Katarzyna Stolarz-Skrzypek, Tatiana Kuznetsova, Lutgarde Thijs, Jan A. Staessen, et al. for the European Project on Genes in Hypertension (EPOGH) Investigators. "Fatal and Nonfatal Outcomes, Incidence of Hypertension, and Blood Pressure Changes in Relation to Urinary Sodium Excretion," JAMA. 4 May 2011, 305(17):1777-1785.

3   David McNemee, "CDC Sodium Intake Guidelines 'Excessively and Unrealistically Low," MedicalNewsToday.com, April 2, 2014. Available at: http://www.medicalnewstoday.com/articles/274856.php.

4   Sabrina Tavernise, "F.D.A. Ruling Would All but Eliminate Trans Fats," The New York Times, November 7, 2013. Available at: http://www.nytimes.com/2013/11/08/health/fda-trans-fats.html?_r=0.

5   Food and Drug Administration. FDA News Release. "FDA Takes Step to Further Reduce Trans Fats in Processed Foods," Food and Drug Administration, November 7, 2013. Available at: http://www.fda.gov/newsevents/newsroom/pressannouncements/ucm373939.htm.

6   Anemona Hartocollis, "Restaurants Prepare for Big Switch: No Trans Fat," The New York Times, June 21, 2008. Available at: http://www.nytimes.com/2008/06/21/nyregion/21trans.html?pagewanted=all.

7   The Hudson Institute, News Release, "Hudson Institute Study: Lower-calorie Foods and Beverages Dramatically Boosted Revenue at 16 Food and Beverage Companies that Account for Nearly $100 billion in Annual Sales," PR Newswire, May 30, 2013. Available at: http://www.prnewswire.com/news-releases/hudson-institute-study-lower-calorie-foods-and-beverages-dramatically-boosted-revenue-at-16-food-and-beverage-companies-that-account-for-nearly-100-billion-in-annual-sales-209684851.html.

8   "Global: Healthy Snacks Market to Grow by Fifth by 2014 – Study." Just Food, September 28, 2010. Available at: http://www.just-food.com/news/healthy-snacks-market-to-grow-by-fifth-by-2014-study_id112603.aspx.

9   Sheri Roan, "Menu Labeling Law Doesn't Register a Blip at Taco Time," The Los Angeles Times, January 14, 2011.

10 Brian Elbel, et al., "Child and Adolescent Fast-Food Choice and the Influence of Calorie Labeling: A Natural Experiment," International Journal of Obesity, February 14, 2011, pp.35, 493-500.

11 Brian Elbel, et al., "Calorie Labeling and Food Choices: A First Look At the Effects on Low-Income People in New York City," Health Affairs, November/December 2009, vol. 28, no. 6, w110-w1121.

12 Shannon Bream, "Supermarkets Cry Foul as FDA Proposes New Food Labeling Rule Under Obamacare," Foxnews.com, February 6, 2013.

13 Ronnie Cohen, "Obesity Rates Remain High, but Stable in the U.S." Reuters,. February 26, 2014.

14 Twatanabe eresa, "Solutions Sought to Reduce Food Waste at Schools," The Los Angeles Times, April 1, 2014.

15 The Tom Douglas Company, "What Our Company is Doing for the Seattle Public Lunch Program," January 6, 2012. Available at: http://tomdouglas.com/blog/2012/01/what-our-company-is-doing-for-the-seattle-public-school-lunch-program/.

16 Erik Mathes, "10 Best School Lunches in America (Slideshow)," The Daily Meal, March 17, 2014. Available at: http://www.thedailymeal.com/10-best-school-lunches-america-slideshow.

17 School Food Focus, School Food 101, "USDA Commodity Foods in School Lunch," Retrieved March 2014 from: http://www.schoolfoodfocus.org/wp-

content/uploads/2010/06/School-Food-101-USDA-Commodity-Foods-in-School-Lunch-FINAL.pdf.
18 *Ibid.*
19 *Ibid.*

CHAPTER 8
1 "Annual Energy Review 2011," Energy Information Administration, September 27, 2012, p. 13. Available at: http://1.usa.gov/1il1w5M.
2 Seamus McGraw, "Is Fracking Safe? The Top 10 Controversial Claims About Natural Gas," *Popular Mechanics,* December 2012, slide 11. Available at: http://bit.ly/1fXaKrZ.
3 "Annual Energy Review 2011," Energy Information Administration, September 27, 2012, p. 89. Available at: http://1.usa.gov/1il1w5M.
4 Samuel T. Pees, "Oil History," *Petrolium History*, 2004. Available at: http://bit.ly/1jVdasl.
5 "Shooters – A 'Fracking' History," American Oil & Gas Historical Society. Available at: http://bit.ly/1lLwE56.
6 Michael MacRae, "Fracking: A Look Back," ASME, December 2012. Avaliable at: http://bit.ly/1ipErAh.
7 Personal interview with Russell Gold, author of *The Boom: How Fracking Ignited the American Energy Revolution and Changed the World*
8 *Ibid.*
9 *Ibid.*
10 Michael MacRae, "Fracking: A Look Back," ASME, December 2012. Avaliable at: http://bit.ly/1ipErAh.
11 Mohammed Aly Sergie, "Hydraulic Fracturing (Fracking)," *Renewing America.* October 15, 2013. Available at: http://on.cfr.org/1ipSDZU.
12 "Abundant Natural Gas Means Low Prices, Increased Trade Potential," IER, April 19, 2012. Available at: http://bit.ly/1jobu9M.
13 Mohammed Aly Sergie, "Hydraulic Fracturing (Fracking)," *Renewing America.* October 15, 2013. Available at: http://on.cfr.org/1ipSDZU.
14 Sean Cockerham, "Fracking-Led Energy Boom Is Turning U.S. into 'Saudi Arabia'," *McClatchy DC*, November 28, 2013. Available at: http://bit.ly/1d2sAWv.
15 "Need a Job? The Oil and Gas Industry Is the Place to Go," Institute for Energy Research, September 6, 2013. Available at: http://bit.ly/PUpJJ9.
16 "Women Making Slow Gains in the Oil and Gas Industry," *Ideas Lab*, March 24, 2014. Available at: http://bit.ly/NQaiAt.
17 Carlton Carroll, "Report: Energy Revolution Creates Career Opportunities for Women and Minorities," American Petroleum Institute, March 5, 2014. Available at: http://bit.ly/1cvhspT.
18 "America's New Energy Future: The Unconventional Oil & Gas Revolution and the US Economy, " IHS. Available at: http://bit.ly/1emBUnX.
19 Jim Efstathiou Jr., "Fracking Boom Seen Raising Household Incomes by $1,200," *Bloomberg*. Available at: http://bloom.bg/1hlWz1r .
20 "U.S. Surges Past Saudis to Become World's Top Oil Supplier –PIRA," *Reuters,* October 15, 2013. Available at: http://reut.rs/1mUzFjS.
21 Suzanne Goldenberg, "US Surpasses Russia as World's Top Oil and Natural Gas Producer," *The Guardian*, October 4, 2013. Available at: http://bit.ly/1caPZnn.
22 "US Exports More Oil Than It Imports For First Time Since 1995," *Al Jazeera*. November 14, 2013. Available at: http://alj.am/1myVshJ.

23 Chris Faulkner, "Russia's Energy Market Is Running on Fumes," *Providence Journal,* February 8, 2014. Available at: http://bit.ly/1fXVtac.

24 Russell Gold, "Rise in U.S. Gas Production Fuels Unexpected Plunge in Emissions," *Wall Street Journal,* April 18, 2013. Available at: http://on.wsj.com/1ocn2Pp.

25 Associated Press, "Natural Gas to Overtake Coal, says ExxonMobil," *Hurriyet Daily News*, Decemember 13, 2013. Available at: http://bit.ly/1ka9Ewr.

26 Russell Gold, "Rise in U.S. Gas Production Fuels Unexpected Plunge in Emissions," *Wall Street Journal,* April 18, 2013. Available at: http://on.wsj.com/1ocn2Pp.

27 "Unprecedented Measurements Provide Better Understanding of Methane Emissions During Natural Gas Production," University of Texas at Austin, September 16, 2014. Available at: http://bit.ly/1iq3oLP.

28 Russell Gold, "Rise in U.S. Gas Production Fuels Unexpected Plunge in Emissions," *Wall Street Journal,* April 18, 2013. Available at: http://on.wsj.com/1ocn2Pp.

29 "Today in Energy," Energy Information Administration, August 1, 2012. Available at: http://1.usa.gov/1kk7yL4.

30 "Fracking: Do the Benefits Derived from Shale Gas Outweigh the Drawbacks of Fracking?" *The Economist,* February 5, 2013. Available at: http://econ.st/1stbj1P.

31 Peter Rugh, "As New York Fracking Moratorium Nears Expiration, Activists Vow to Take Action," *Waging Nonviolence*, January 11, 2013. Available at: http://bit.ly/1qeQoO7.

32 Personal interview with Cabot spokesperson.

33 Seamus McGraw, "Is Fracking Safe? The Top 10 Controversial Claims About Natural Gas," *Popular Mechanics,* December 2012, slide 11. Available at: http://bit.ly/1fXaKrZ.

34 Catherine Tsai, "Halliburton Executive Drinks Fracking Fluid At Conference," *The Huffington Post,* August 22, 2011. Available at: http://huff.to/1iq6UWC.

35 Ben Wolfgang, "I Drank Fracking Fluid, Says Colorado Gov. John Hickenlooper," *The Washington Times,* February 12, 2013. Available at: http://bit.ly/1g1y3xf.

36 EnergyInDepth, Video: "EPA's Lisa Jackson on safe hydraulic fracturing," YouTube, April 30,2012. Available at: http://bit.ly/1iq7TWE.

37 EnergyInDepth, Video: "EPA Administrator Lisa Jackson Tells Congress 'No Proven Cases Where Fracking Has Affected Water," YouTube, May 24, 2011. Available at: http://bit.ly/1mVNP1g.

38 Ben Geman, "Energy Secretary: Natural Gas Helps Battle Climate Change – for Now," *The Hill.* August 1, 2013. Available at: http://bit.ly/1h9lNPz.

39 Steve Everley, "How Anti-Fracking Activists Deny Science: Water Contamination," *EnergyInDepth,* August 13, 2013. Available at: http://bit.ly/PHexjd.

40 "FAQ: What Is U.S. Electricity Generation by Energy Source?" Energy Information Administration. May 9, 2013. Available at: http://1.usa.gov/1fhXKfE.

41 Sterling Burnett, "New Report: Green Energy Technology Not Ready for Prime Time," NCPA, October 24, 2013. Available at: http://bit.ly/1qeSFsG.

42 "Energy Department Announces $60 Million to Drive Affordable, Efficient Solar Power," US Department of Energy, October 22, 2013. Available at: http://1.usa.gov/1g1C19g.

43 Ryan Tracy, "Some Clean-Energy Loans Raise Red Flags," *Wall Street Journal,* March 23, 2012. Available at: http://on.wsj.com/1kDNvD2.

44 Michael Bastasch, "CBO: Most Energy Tax Subsidies Go Toward Green Energy, Energy Efficiency," *Daily Caller,* March 14, 2013. Available at: http://bit.ly/1hxXTIG.

45 Chart available at: http://1.usa.gov/1iigDy3.

46 "The Energy Subsidy Tally," *The Wall Street Journal.* Available at: http://online.wsj.com/news/articles/SB1000142405311190328570457655910357367 3300.

47 "IER Testimony for the Kansas Senate Standing Committee on Utilities," IER, March 19, 2014. Available at: http://bit.ly/1qg6hC2.

48 Daniel Kish, "End the Wind Production Tax Credit," Institute for Energy Research. Available at: http://www.usnews.com/opinion/blogs/on-energy/2012/12/13/end-the-wind-production-tax-credit.

49 "Powering Down the Wind Subsidy," T*he Wall Street Journal.* Available at: http://online.wsj.com/news/articles/SB10001424052702304854804579236 200486481022

50 "The Status of Renewable Electricity Mandates in the States," The Institute for Energy Research. Available at: http://www.instituteforenergyresearch.org/wp-content/uploads/2010/12/IER-RPS-Study-one-pager.pdf.

51 "The Ethanol Tax," *The Wall Street Journal.* Available at: http://online.wsj.com/news/articles/SB10001424127887323309404578611842837454104.

52 "Even the U.N. Hates Ethanol," *The Wall Street Journal.* Available at: http://online.wsj.com/news/articles/SB10001424052702303848104576383712876 710474.

53 "The Cellulosic Ethanol Debacle," *The Wall Street Journal.* Available at: http://online.wsj.com/news/articles/SB10001424052970204012004577072 470158115782.

54 Fred Upton, "Keystone XL #TimetoBuild." Available at: http://energycommerce.house.gov/content/keystone-xl.

55 "Final Supplemental Environmental Impact Statement for the Keystone XL Pipeline." The U.S. Department of State, Bureau of Oceans and International Environment and Scientific Affairs. Available at: http://www.documentcloud.org/documents/1011311-keystone-report.html#document/p1.

CHAPTER 9

1 Telework Research Network. Available at: http://www.teleworkresearchnetwork.com/telecommuting-statistics.

2 *Ibid.*

3 "Commuting in the United States: 2009," U.S. Census Bureau, September 2011. Available at: http://www.census.gov/prod/2011pubs/acs-15.pdf.

4 "One-third of Married Couples in U.S. Meet Online: Study," *New York Daily News*, June 4, 2013. Available at: http://www.nydailynews.com/life-style/one-third-u-s-marriages-start-online-dating-study-article-1.1362743.

5 U.S. Census Bureau, "Quarterly Retail E-Commerce Sales," February 18, 2014. Available at: https://www.census.gov/retail/mrts/www/data/pdf/ec_current.pdf.

6 Francesco Di Lorenzo and Pietro Paganini, "2013 International Property Rights Index," Property Rights Alliance, October 29, 2013. Available at: http://www.propertyrightsalliance.org/property-rights-gdp-growth-positively-linked-a3034.

7 Paul Misener, Testimony before the House Judiciary Committee's subcommittee on Courts, Intellectual Property and the Internet, November 19, 2013. Available at: http://judiciary.house.gov/_files/hearings/113th/11192013/111913%20Testimony%20Misener.pdf.

8   John McCoskey, Testimony before the House Judiciary Committee's subcommittee on Courts, Intellectual Property and the Internet, November 19, 2013. Available at: http://judiciary.house.gov/_files/hearings/113th/11192013/111913%20Testimony%20McCoskey.pdf.

9   Carrie Lukas, "Protecting Intellectual Property: A Key to Growth and Progress," Independent Women's Forum, June 4, 2014. Available at: http://iwf.org/blog/2791434/Protecting-Intellectual-Property:--A-Key-to-Growth-and-Progress.

10   Matthew Herper, "The Truly Staggering Cost Of Inventing New Drugs," *Forbes*, February 10, 2012. Available at: http://www.forbes.com/sites/matthewherper/2012/02/10/the-truly-staggering-cost-of-inventing-new-drugs/.

11   "Exposing One of China's Cyber Espionage Units," Mandiant, 2013. Available at: http://intelreport.mandiant.com/Mandiant_APT1_Report.pdf.

12   Carrie Lukas, "It's Time for the U.S. to Deal with Cyber-Espionage," *U.S. News and World Report*, June 4, 2013. Available at: http://www.iwf.org/news/2791435/It's-Time-for-the-U.S.-to-Deal-with-Cyber-Espionage#sthash.CD9ZTJdn.dpuf.

13   "Cybersecurity: National Strategy, Roles, and Responsibilities Need to Be Better Defined and More Effectively Implemented," General Accounting Office, February 2013. Available at : http://www.gao.gov/assets/660/652170.pdf.

14   Mywireless.com, 2013 National Tax Survey. Available at: http://www.mywireless.org/media-center/data-center/2013-national-tax-survey/.

15   Mywireless.com. Available at: http://www.mywireless.org/state-issues/.

16   Mywireless.com, 2013 National Tax Survey. Available at: http://www.mywireless.org/media-center/data-center/2013-national-tax-survey/.

CHAPTER 10

1   2010 Annual Social and Economic Supplements from the Current Population Survey, U.S. Census Bureau, 2011. Defined as $22,113 for a family of four in 2010.

2   The United States Department of Agriculture. Available at: http://www.fns.usda.gov/pd/SNAPsummary.htm.

3   Economic News Release, "Table A-15, Alternative Measures of Labor Under-utilization," Bureau of Labor Statistics, May 2, 2014. Available at: http://www.bls.gov/news.release/empsit.t15.htm.

4   Generation Opportunity News Release, "Youth Unemployment at 15.8% in February," March 2014. Available at: http://generationopportunity.org/press/youth-unemployment-at-15-8-in-february/#axzz2xTbVfAjW.

5   National Alliance to End Homelessness, "Snapshot of Homelessness." Available at: http://www.endhomelessness.org/pages/snapshot_of_homelessness.

6   Mary Kate Cary, "The Shocking Truth on Entitlements," *U.S. News & World Report,* December 2012. Available at: http://www.usnews.com/opinion/articles/2012/12/19/the-shocking-truth-on-entitlements .

7   Congressional Budget Office, Growth in Means-Tested Programs and Tax Credits for Low-Income Households, February 11, 2013. Available at: http://www.cbo.gov/publication/43934.

8   Stephanie J. Ventura, "Changing Patterns of Nonmarital Childbearing in the United States," Center for Disease Control, NCHS Data Brief No. 18, May 2009. Available at: http://www.cdc.gov/nchs/data/databriefs/db18.pdf.

9   Sara S. McLanahan, "The Consequences of Nonmarital Childbearing for Women, Children, and Society," *Report to Congress on Out-of-Wedlock Childbearing*, September 1995. Available at: http://www.cdc.gov/nchs/data/misc/wedlock.pdf.

10   Raj Chetty, et al. "Where is the Land of Opportunity? The Geography of Intergenerational Mobility in the United States," National Bureau of Economic Research, January 2014. Available at: http://obs.rc.fas.harvard.edu/chetty/mobility_geo.pdf.
11   USDA Food and Nutrition Service, Supplemental Assistance Nutrition Program, April 4, 2014. Available at: http://www.fns.usda.gov/pd/34snapmonthly.htm.
12   *Ibid.*
13   Robert Rector and Katherine Bradley, "Reforming the Food Stamp Program," Heritage Background #2708, July 2012. Available at: http://www.heritage.org/research/reports/2012/07/reforming-the-food-stamp-program.
14   "Sequester Replacement Reconciliation Act of 2012," Report of the Committee on the Budget, Report 112-470, U.S. House of Representatives, to Accompany H.R. 5652, 112th Cong., 2nd Sess., May 9, 2012, p. 20. Available at: http://www.gpo.gov/fdsys/pkg/CRPT-112hrpt470/pdf/CRPT-112hrpt470.pdf.
15   Robert Rector and Katherine Bradley, "Reforming the Food Stamp Program," Heritage Background #2708, July 2012, p. 52, Table A16. Available at: http://www.heritage.org/research/reports/2012/07/reforming-the-food-stamp-program#_ftn25.
16   Robert Rector and Katherine Bradley, "Reforming the Food Stamp Program," Heritage Background #2708, July 2012. Available at: http://www.heritage.org/research/reports/2012/07/reforming-the-food-stamp-program#_ftn25.
17   Robert Rector, "An Overview of Obama's End Run on Welfare Reform," Heritage Foundation Issue Brief #3735, September 20, 2012. Available at: http://www.heritage.org/research/reports/2012/09/an-overview-of-obamas-end-run-on-welfare-reform.
18   Rukmalie Jayakody, Sheldon Danziger, and Harold Pollack, "Welfare Reform, Substance Abuse and Mental Health," *Journal of Health Politics, Policy and Law,* Vol. 25, No. 4, August 2000, pp. 623–652.
19   Michael Tanner and Charles Hughes, "The Work Versus Welfare Trade-off: 2013 An Analysis of the Total Level of Welfare Benefits by State," Cato Institute, 2013. Available at: http://object.cato.org/sites/cato.org/files/pubs/pdf/the_work_versus_welfare_trade-off_2013_wp.pdf.
20   Medicaid.gov. Available at : http://www.medicaid.gov/Medicaid-CHIP-Program-Information/By-Topics/Eligibility/Eligibility.html.
21   Alan B. Krueger and Andreas Mueller, "Job Search and Unemployment Insurance: New Evidence from Time Use Data," IZA Discussion Paper No. 3667, August 2008, p. 11. Available at: http://ssrn.com/abstract=1261452.
22   Social Security Administration. Available at: http://www.ssa.gov/cgi-bin/currentpay.cgi.
23   Carrie Lukas, "Yes America, Your Fellow Citizens DO Abuse Federal Aid Programs," Forbes, October 2, 2012. Available at: http://www.iwf.org/news/2789418/Yes-America,-Your-Fellow-Citizens-DO-Abuse-Federal-Aid-Programs.
24   "2014 Annual Report: Additional Opportunities to Reduce Fragmentation, Overlap, and Duplication and Achieve Other Financial Benefits, " General Accounting Office, GAO-14-343SP, April 2014. Available at: http://www.gao.gov/products/GAO-14-343SP#mt=e-report&st=2.
25   Anne Lowrey, "Ending Poverty by Giving to the Poor." *New York Times,* June 20, 2013. Available at: http://economix.blogs.nytimes.com/2013/06/20/ending-poverty-by-giving-the-poor-money/?_php=true&_type=blogs&_r=0.

CHAPTER 11

1   "Table B-1. Employees on nonfarm payrolls by industry sector and selected industry detail," Economic News Release, Bureau of Labor Statistics, May 2, 2014. Available at: http://www.bls.gov/news.release/empsit.t17.htm.

2   "Monthly Statistical Snapshot, March 2014," Social Security Administration, May 2014. Available at: http://www.socialsecurity.gov/policy/docs/quickfacts/stat_snapshot/.

3   Fast Facts, Social Security Administration. Available at: http://www.socialsecurity.gov/policy/docs/chartbooks/fast_facts/2011/fast_facts11.html.

4   Fast Facts, Social Security Administration. Available at: http://www.socialsecurity.gov/policy/docs/chartbooks/fast_facts/2011/fast_facts11.html.

5   "A Summary of the 2013 Annual Reports," Social Security and Medicare Boards of Trustees, 2013. Available at: http://www.socialsecurity.gov/OACT/TRSUM/index.html.

6   "A Summary of the 2013 Annual Reports," Social Security and Medicare Boards of Trustees, 2013. Available at: http://www.socialsecurity.gov/OACT/TRSUM/index.html.

7   "The Underfunding of State and Local Pension Plans," Congressional Budget Office, Economic and Budget Issue Brief, May 2011.

8   U.S. Census Bureau, "Life Expectancy at Birth and at Age 65 by Sex—Selected Countries: 1990 and 2007," Table 1339. Available at: http://www.census.gov/compendia/statab/2011/tables/11s1339.pdf.

9   Charles Blahous, "Don't Worsen Social Security's Soaring Cost Problem," E21 Morning Ebrief, December 23, 2014. Available at: http://www.economics21.org/commentary/don%E2%80%99t-worsen-social-security%E2%80%99s-soaring-cost-problem.

10 For a discussion of options, see Charles Blahous, *Social Security: The Unfinished Work*, Hoover Institute Press, Nov 2010.

11 See Social Security Administration. Available at: http://www.socialsecurity.gov/policy/docs/quickfacts/prog_highlights/.

12 Michael Tanner, "Bankrupt: Entitlements and the Federal Budget," Cato Institute Policy Analysis 673, March 28, 2011. Available at: http://www.cato.org/sites/cato.org/files/pubs/pdf/pa673.pdf.

13 Patrick McGuinn, "Pension Politics: Public Employee Retirement System Reform in Four States," Brookings Institute, February 2014. Available at: http://www.brookings.edu/~/media/research/files/papers/2014/02/26%20public%20pension%20reform/pension%20politics_final_225.pdf.

14 Stephen F. Hayes, "On, Wisconsin!," Weekly Standard, Volume 17, No. 36, June 4, 2012.

15 Angela Johnson, "76% of Americans are living paycheck-to-paycheck," CNN Mondy, June 24, 2013. Available at: http://money.cnn.com/2013/06/24/pf/emergency-savings/.

16 Abby Schachter, "MyRA," Independent Women's Forum Policy Focus, March 2014. Available at: http://c1355372.cdn.cloudfiles.rackspacecloud.com/0acdf410-729d-406a-b552-db5586a1a448/PolicyFocus14_March_p2.pdf.

CHAPTER 12

1   Ruth Marcus, "What the Duke Porn-Star Student Shows Us about Our Degraded Culture," *The Washington Post*, March 12, 2014. Available at: http://www.washingtonpost.com/opinions/ruth-marcus-the-duke-porn-star-students-degrading-plan-to-pay-tuition/2014/03/11/b70c96a4-a940-11e3-b61e-8051b8b52d06_story.html.

2   Doris J. James, "Profile of Jail Inmates," United States Department of Justice, Bureau of Juvenile Statistics Special Report, NCJ 201932, Washington D.C., United States Government Printing Office, 2002, p.1.

3   Wisconsin Division of Youth Services, "Family Status of Delinquents in Juvenile Correctional Facilities in Wisconsin," 1994.

4   Kay Hymowitz. "The Real, Complex Relation Between Single-Parent Families and Crime," *The Atlantic,* Dec. 3, 2012. Available at: http://www.theatlantic.com/sexes/archive/2012/12/the-real-complex-connection-between-single-parent-families-and-crime/265860/

5   George F. Will, "Paul Ryan Was Right—Poverty is a Cultural Problem," *The Washington Post,* March 21, 2014. Available at: http://www.washingtonpost.com/opinions/george-f-will-the-lefts-half-century-of-denial-over-poverty/2014/03/21/1aeaff4e-b049-11e3-a49e-76adc9210f19_story.html.

6   "The Negro Family: The Case for National Action," Office of Policy Planning and Research, United States Department of Labor, March 1965. Available at: http://www.dol.gov/oasam/programs/history/webid-meynihan.htm.

7   Nick Shultz, *Home Economics: The Consequences of Changing the Family Structure,* AEI Press, March 16, 2013.

8   Carrie Lukas, *The Politically Incorrect Guide to Women, Sex, and Feminism,* Regnery Publishing, May 2006.

9   Steven F. Hayward, *The Age of Reason: The Fall of the Old Liberal Order, 1964-1980,* New York, Three Rivers Press, 2001.

10 Kay Hymowitz, *Marriage and Caste in America: Separate and Unequal Families in a Post-Marital Age,* Ivan E. Ree Publisher, 2006.

11 Charles Murray, *Coming Apart,* Crown Forum, New York, 2012, p. 132.

12 Avik Roy, "How Americans Game the $200 Billion-a-Year 'Disability Industrial Complex," *Forbes,* April 8, 2013. Available at: http://www.forbes.com/sites/theapothecary/2013/04/08/how-americans-game-the-200-billion-a-year-disability-industrial-complex/.

13 Charles Murray, *Coming Apart,* Crown Forum, New York, 2012.

14 W. Bradford Wilcox, et al., *Why Marriage Matters,* Center for Marriage and Families, 3rd edition, 2011.

15 Arthur C. Brooks, "Be Open-Handed Toward Your Brothers: A Conservative Social Justice Agenda," *Commentary,* April 2014, pp. 13-21.

16 "Millions of Americans Forced to Work Part-Time," CBS This Morning: Saturday, April 14, 2014.

17 Thomas Jefferson, *Notes on the State of Virginia. Query XIX. 1789,* Electronic Text, University of Virginia Library. Available at: http://web.archive.org/web/20110221131434/http://etext.lib.virginia.edu/etcbin/toccer-new2?id=JefVirg.sgm&images=images/modeng&data=/texts/english/modeng/parsed&tag=public&part=19&division=div1.

ABOUT THE AUTHORS

CARRIE LUKAS
(Introduction, Chapters Nine and Eleven, and Conclusion)

Carrie is managing director of the Independent Women's Forum. She is the co-author of *Liberty Is No War on Women*, author of *The Politically Incorrect Guide to Women, Sex, and Feminism*, and a contributor to Forbes.com. She has a B.A. from Princeton and a master's in public policy from Harvard University. She is married with four children.

SABRINA SCHAEFFER
(Introduction, Chapter Four, and Conclusion)

Sabrina is executive director of the Independent Women's Forum. Previously she was managing partner of Evolving Strategies. She is the co-author of *Liberty Is No War on Women*, and a contributor to Forbes.com, *The Hill*, and Ricochet and a regular panelist on the Fox New Channel's "Forbes on Fox" every week. She has a B.A. from Middlebury College and M.A.s in American history and politics from the University of Virginia. She is married with three children.

DIANA FURCHTGOTT-ROTH
Chapter One

Diana, former chief economist of the U.S. Department of Labor, is a senior fellow and director of Economics21 at the Manhattan Institute for Policy Research. She served as chief of staff of President George W. Bush's Council of Economic Advisers. She is the author of *Women's Figures: An Illustrated Guide to the Economic Progress of Women in America* and a columnist for MarketWatch. com. She received her B.A. in economics from Swarthmore College and her M.Phil. in economics from Oxford University.

ROMINA BOCCIA
Chapter Two

Romina is the Grover M. Hermann Fellow in Federal Budgetary Affairs at the Heritage Foundation. Before working at Heritage, she was a policy analyst at the Independent Women's Forum. She received her B.S. and her master's degree in economics from George Mason University. Romina, who was born and grew up in Augsburg, Germany, currently resides with her husband in Clinton, Md.

HADLEY HEATH MANNING
Chapter Three

Hadley is the director of health policy at the Independent Women's Forum. She has been a National Review Institute Washington Fellow, and is a contributor to Doublethink Magazine and Red Alert Politics. She has a B.A. in economics and journalism from the University of North Carolina. She lives with her husband in Denver, Colorado.

VICKI ALGER
Chapters Five and Six

Vicki is a senior fellow at the Independent Women's Forum and a Research Fellow at the Independent Institute. She has held education directorships at the Pacific Research Institute and the Goldwater Institute. Vicki received her Ph.D. in political philosophy from the University of Dallas, where she was an Earhart Foundation Fellow. She currently lives in Scottsdale, Arizona, with her husband and four stepsons.

JULIE GUNLOCK
Chapter Seven

Julie Gunlock is the director of the Culture of Alarmism Project at the Independent Women's Forum and the author of *From Chemicals to Cupcakes: How the Culture of Alarmism Makes Us Afraid of Everything and How to Fight Back*. Before joining IWF, Gunlock served as a Professional Staff Member on the Senate Homeland Security Committee, and on the staffs of Ohio Senators Mike DeWine and George Voinovich. She is married with three sons.

JILLIAN MELCHIOR
Chapter Eight

Jillian is a senior fellow at the Independent Women's Forum and covers energy and environmental issues. She also writes for National Review as a Thomas L. Rhodes Fellow for the Franklin Center for Government and Public Integrity. She was a 2011 Robert Novak fellow for the Phillips Foundation, and is a graduate of Hillsdale College.

PATRICE J. LEE
Chapter Ten

Patrice is a senior fellow at the Independent Women's Forum and Director of Outreach at Generation Opportunity where she works to promote economic opportunity for Millennials. She earned her bachelor's degree in economics and political science from Tufts University and a master's degree in international relations from Boston College.

CHARLOTTE HAYS
Chapter Twelve

Charlotte Hays is senior editor and director of cultural programs at the Independent Women's Forum. She first joined the IWF in 1999 as editor of *The Women's Quarterly*. Her work has appeared in the *Wall Street Journal*, *New York Magazine*, the *Washington Post*'s "Book World," and the *Weekly Standard*. Charlotte is also a coauthor of three humorous books on southern culture.

ABOUT

*i*ndependent™
women'sforum

The Independent Women's Forum's mission is to improve the lives of Americans by increasing the number of women who value free markets and personal liberty. IWF is a non-partisan, 501(c)(3) research and educational institution. By aggressively seeking earned media, providing easy-to-read, timely publications and commentary, and reaching out to the public, we seek to cultivate support for these important principles and encourage women to join us in working to return the country to limited, Constitutional government.

13842029R10131

Made in the USA
San Bernardino, CA
08 August 2014